POLICY PAPERS IN

INTERNATIONAL AFFAIRS

*

NUMBER THIRTEEN

CUBA'S POLICY IN AFRICA, 1959-1980

WILLIAM M. LeoGRANDE

INSTITUTE OF INTERNATIONAL STUDIES
UNIVERSITY OF CALIFORNIA
BERKELEY

In sponsoring the Policy Papers in International Affairs series, the Institute of International Studies reasserts its commitment to a vigorous policy debate by providing a forum for innovative approaches to important policy issues. The views expressed in each paper are those of the author only, and publication in this series does not constitute endorsement by the Institute.

International Standard Book Number 0-87725-513-X

Library of Congress Card Number 80-52088

CONTENTS

CONTENTS

LIST OF TABLES

ACKNOWLEDGMENTS

For their valuable comments on the initial draft of this manuscript, the author would like to thank Professors John Marcum and Kenneth Jowitt. Portions of Chapters I-IV appeared originally in *Cuban Studies*, and the author wishes to express his appreciation to Editor Carmelo Mesa-Lago for permission to incorporate that material here. Finally, thanks to Mr. Paul Gilchrist, who edited the entire manuscript.

W.M.L.

Washington, D.C. 1980

INTRODUCTION

Caught in the crossfire of the cold war, the Cuban revolution spent its first decade trying to survive. Apart from Cuba's relations with the Soviet Union, which it cultivated as a necessary condition of survival, Cuban foreign policy, like the foreign policy of most small states, was regional rather than global. The Cubans did, of course, have relations further afield, but the focus of policy was in the Western Hemisphere, where Cuba sought to break the diplomatic and economic isolation imposed on it by the United States by promoting revolutions throughout the region. When this strategy met with little success, Cuba adopted a more conciliatory and pragmatic attitude toward its Latin American neighbors. Thus the sudden appearance of Cuban combat troops in Africa in 1975 came as a rude shock to the United States; the regional pariah had, seemingly overnight, become a global actor. The specter of Cuba spreading revolution in Latin America—a fear that dominated U.S. policy in the Western Hemisphere for over a decade—suddenly loomed over the whole of the Third World.

Though the major commitment of Cuban combat troops to Africa appears to be a radical departure in Cuban foreign policy, this new activism is quite consistent with earlier policies toward Africa—policies whose roots can be traced to the earliest years of the Cuban revolution. What has changed is the international environment, prompting Cuban actions which differ strikingly from the actions undertaken in the 1960s, but designed to promote the same basic foreign policy objectives.

There are four essential differences between Cuba's recent initiatives in Africa and its behavior during the 1960s. First, the "internationalist" dimension of Cuban policy is given greater emphasis than ever before. Throughout its first decade, the Cuban revolution's first priority internationally was survival in the face of intense U.S. hostility. As the U.S. threat has receded in the 1970s, the relative security enjoyed by the revolutionary regime has enabled it to concentrate greater energy on expanding Cuban influence in the Third World and on providing assistance to movements and governments it regards as progressive.

1

The second difference in Cuban policy concerns the instrumentalities through which this internationalist policy is implemented. Cuban international assistance has always had two operational components: aid to guerrilla movements fighting colonial or neocolonial regimes and aid to progressive governments. During the 1960s Cuba emphasized aid to guerrillas, especially—but not exclusively—in Latin America. This focus related directly to Cuba's preoccupation with the U.S. threat: aid to guerrillas or friendly governments outside the Western Hemisphere was marginal to its overriding security concern. In the 1970s, however, Cuban international assistance has shifted its operational emphasis from aiding guerrillas to aiding progressive governments, and its geographical emphasis from Latin America to Africa. While these changes are rooted in Cuba's improved security situation, they also reflect the failures of Latin American guerrillas, the Cuban belief that the United States will not tolerate "another Cuba" in the Western Hemisphere, and the special opportunities provided to African revolutionaries by the collapse of Portuguese colonialism.

The third policy difference is the large-scale commitment of regular Cuban combat troops abroad. While the deployment of Cuban combat troops is not unprecedented (Cuba sent troops to Algeria in 1963 and to Syria in 1973), the size of the commitments to Angola (1975) and Ethiopia (1978) marks a new departure in Cuban military assistance. The dispatch of large numbers of troops was impossible in the 1960s, when they were needed at home to protect the island against a possible U.S. attack, and when Cuban relations with the USSR were not friendly enough to make cooperative military ventures feasible.

The fourth difference in Cuba's foreign policy concerns its relations with the USSR. Cuban-Soviet relations have grown especially close since 1970. The virtual identity of Cuban and Soviet views on the global situation makes possible a coordination of Cuban and Soviet policy—in Africa and elsewhere—that enables Cuba to project its military capabilities abroad to a much greater extent than if it were acting alone.

I

CUBAN-SOVIET RELATIONS AND
CUBAN FOREIGN POLICY, 1959-1975

Cuba has never fit the model of Soviet satellite so often depicted in early polemics by the revolution's opponents, and recently resurrected by critics of Cuba's African policy. Though its relationship with the USSR has been Cuba's most important bilateral connection since 1961, it has been a complex and often tense relationship. The economic, military, political, and ideological facets of Cuban-Soviet relations have varied tremendously over the past two decades, and have not always been in harmony with one another.[1]

In the 1960s the very survival of the Cuban revolution depended upon establishing and maintaining a close economic and military relationship with the USSR. Faced with the unmitigated hostility of the United States—hostility which took the form of both military and economic sanctions—the revolutionary government's life was very much at stake. Alignment with the USSR meant Soviet arms to defend the island against conventional attack, a "nuclear umbrella" to deter full-scale U.S. intervention, and economic assistance to rescue an economy so dependent on the United States that it could not otherwise have survived the severance of U.S.-Cuban economic ties. The determination of Cuba's revolutionary leaders to break U.S. political and economic hegemony over the island could only be realized by realigning Cuba toward the USSR, and the maintenance of that new alignment—both economic and military—was (and is) a necessary condition of the survival of the revolution.

With Cuba forced to rely upon Soviet assistance to survive, it is not surprising that Cuban-Soviet relations have been extremely tense when Cuba's leaders have had reason to doubt the Soviet Union's commitment to the island. The 1962 "Cuban missile crisis" was the first such occasion. Wanting to keep the partially installed Soviet IRBM's to deter a U.S. invasion of the island, Cuba was unyielding in the crisis, but Khrushchev, recognizing the inferiority of the Soviet's strategic nuclear position, proceeded to negotiate an end to the crisis without consulting the Cubans. Enraged, Cuba refused to allow the on-site inspections which the United States and the USSR had agreed to as a means of verifying the removal of the Soviet missiles. Cuban-Soviet relations deteriorated sharply. No longer trusting the USSR to defend its revolution, Cuba moved to reduce the U.S. threat directly by trying to ease tensions with its northern neighbor. Initial contacts with the United States were interrupted by Kennedy's assassination, and the possibility of rapprochement evaporated as the United States escalated the war in Vietnam. The legacy of the missile crisis remained, however: never again would Cuba place unlimited faith in Soviet support. Cuba's leaders had clearly learned that the Soviet Union's assistance was conditioned by the overall structure of Soviet foreign policy objectives.

The perennial danger for Cuba in its relationship with the USSR was the lack of tangible benefits to the Soviets. After failing in its 1962 gambit to install IRBM's in Cuba, the USSR was forced to settle for relatively modest political benefits purchased at considerable material cost. As the "first free territory of the Americas," Cuba was a potential model for anti-imperialist revolution in the rest of the Western Hemisphere (where the Soviet influence was neglible) and in the Third World generally, but attempts at imitation in the 1960s invariably came to naught.

On the other side of the ledger, the costs borne by the Soviets were considerable. In addition to funding Cuba's economy and its military establishment, the Soviets had to bear significant political costs. Cuba's stubborn independence in both domestic and foreign policy contributed to a growing polycentricism in the socialist camp, further undermining the Soviets' claim to leadership, while the persistent friction between Cuba and the United States complicated Soviet relations with its superpower rival. The burden of such costs, when balanced against the USSR's modest gains from its relationship with Cuba, raises the question of why the Soviet Union chose to maintain the relationship. The central explanation lies in a basic doctrine of Soviet foreign policy: the irreversibility of socialist revolutions. Once the Soviets acknowledged Cuba's socialist character, they were committed to the revolution's survival—whatever the cost. In all likelihood, Cuba also benefitted from the cautiousness of the Soviet leadership that replaced Khrushchev in 1964. Foreign policy failures were a major factor in Khrushchev's demise; not only had he lost the missile crisis confrontation, but he had also presided over the great schism in the socialist camp—the Sino-Soviet split. It is doubtful that the new leadership would have risked a break with the

Cubans, thereby opening themselves to the charge of having "lost Cuba."

Finally, Cuba in the 1960s was the premier example of a successful national liberation struggle. Support of such struggles had become a major focus of Soviet politico-military competition with the West in the era of mutual deterrence. A Soviet break with Cuba would have undermined the Soviet position as a supporter of national liberation movements and lent credence to China's charges that the Soviets were no longer pursuing a revolutionary foreign policy. In short, while the Soviet Union enjoyed only meager benefits from its relationship with Cuba, the cost of terminating the relationship far outweighed the cost of maintaining it.

For Cuba, however, such a calculus was at best an uncertain foundation for the island's security. Soviet-Cuban relations developed their most serious strains in the mid-1960s. The bitterness of 1962-1963 had resulted from Soviet behavior in the critical situation of the missile crisis; the animosity of 1966-1968 stemmed from more fundamental differences between the two nations.

By 1966, Cuban leaders had rejected both the Soviet model for the construction of socialism domestically and the "peaceful coexistence" posture of Soviet policy internationally, especially as it related to the war in Vietnam. While the USSR experimented with economic reforms that relied upon limited market relations, Cuba was entering the period of revolutionary *conciencia*. Moral incentives replaced material ones in a full-scale effort to create "new socialist man": Cuba was going to build socialism and communism simultaneously. From this lofty perspective, the Soviet reforms looked suspiciously like a reversion to capitalism.[2]

Soviet foreign policy was even more troubling to Cuba. Not only did peaceful coexistence seem unjustified, but the USSR's dogged pursuit of it despite the U.S. escalation in Vietnam deeply worried Cuba.[3] If the United States was willing to expend such efforts in far off Vietnam, might it not turn its military force on Cuba next? Could the USSR be relied upon to defend Cuba at the expense of peaceful coexistence? Soviet policy toward the Third World seemed increasingly unrevolutionary. In Latin America the USSR was willing to conduct normal relations with states observing the Organization of American States' (OAS) sanctions against Cuba, and in Africa it had retreated from its early policy of substantial aid commitments to progressive African regimes.[4]

Unsure of Soviet military commitments because of Vietnam and unsure of Soviet economic aid because of doubts about the quality of Soviet socialism, Cuba sought to ensure its security by reducing its dependence on the USSR. A new radical foreign policy emerged, with two strategic objectives: (1) to spark revolution in Latin America, thus ending Cuba's hemispheric isolation and also easing pressure on Vietnam because the United States would be forced to deal with "two, three, many Vietnams," and (2) to form a third force within the socialist camp composed of Cuba, Vietnam, and North Korea to promote militant socialist solidarity in the face of U.S. aggression.

From the Cuban perspective, revolution in Latin America promised a variety of salutary effects. It would break Cuba's diplomatic and economic isolation in the hemisphere, thereby reducing its economic dependence on the USSR. By providing Cuba with military allies (who might make up in numbers what they lacked in strength), it would improve Cuban security. Finally, a revolutionary upsurge in Latin America would force a U.S. response, straining U.S. military capabilities and thereby easing the pressure on Vietnam.

The formation of a third force of militant front-line states within the socialist camp was intended to stiffen the spine of Soviet policymakers who seemed intent on pursuing peaceful coexistence despite Vietnam's agony. At the very least, it would confront the Soviets with *several* states advocating a more militant policy, thereby reducing the probability of any Soviet sanctions against such dissidence.

Neither of Cuba's objectives was attained. Despite a surge in Cuban aid to Latin American guerrillas between 1966 and 1968, few of the insurgent movements proved to be a match for U.S.-trained and equipped counterinsurgency forces scattered throughout the hemisphere. After Che Guevara's death in Bolivia, Cuban enthusiasm for the "export" of revolution waned considerably, and Cuban criticisms of the USSR's lack of revolutionary internationalism were greatly moderated.

The reduced Cuban criticism of the USSR may also have been due in part to Soviet economic pressure. In early 1968, Soviet petroleum deliveries to Cuba were delayed. The USSR maintained that the problem was merely logistical, and Cuba has never publicly disputed this explanation, though most observers have interpreted the delay as politically motivated.[5] Whatever the cause, the incident served to emphasize the dependence of the Cuban economy on the USSR.

Reconciliation between Cuba and the Soviet Union came about dramatically in August 1968 when Castro endorsed the Soviet intervention in Czechoslovakia.[6] Two considerations probably prompted the Cuban leadership's decision. First, Dubček's reforms were even further removed from Cuba's model of socialist development than the modest Soviet reforms that Cuba had been criticizing since 1966. Thus the Soviet charge that socialism in Czechoslovakia was endangered by Dubček was probably credible to the Cubans. In that case, from the Cuban perspective, some sort of Soviet action was not only justified but mandated. Since the principle of the irreversibility of socialist revolutions, and the willingness of the USSR to risk international crisis and opprobrium to support that principle, were the linchpin of Cuban national security, the Cubans probably viewed the Soviet intervention more with reassurance than with trepidation.

From 1968 to 1972 Cuban foreign policy was eclipsed by prodigious domestic problems associated with the drive to produce 10 million tons of sugar in 1970. When that crisis had passed and foreign policy emerged from the shadow of domestic concerns, Cuba faced a world considerably different from that of the 1960s. Consequently, though Cuba's basic foreign policy objectives remained unchanged, the specific policies adopted to pursue those objectives were quite different. One crucial difference was the evolution of a close Cuban-Soviet relationship between 1970 and 1972. By 1970 it was clear that Cuba's "great leap" approach to development had failed, and its subsequent economic reforms brought Cuba much closer to the Soviet model of socialist construction, eliminating a major source of Cuban-Soviet friction in the mid-1960s. The improvement in Cuban-Soviet relations was also facilitated by increases in Soviet economic aid during the difficult years of 1971 and 1972, which culminated with Cuba joining the Council for Mutual Economic Assistance (CMEA or Comecon) in 1972 as a full member.[7] While this closer economic relationship with Cuba and the USSR could be viewed as increasing Cuban dependence, it also had the effect of reducing the likelihood that Soviet assistance would be withdrawn.

As one of the focal points of East-West hostilities during the 1960s, Cuba was deeply affected by the global transition from cold war to detente. The easing of international tensions, together with the U.S. defeat in Vietnam, greatly reduced the threat of U.S. military action against Cuba. It also stimulated political pressures for an end to sanctions against Cuba both in the United States and in the OAS. In the early 1970s a number of Latin American nations ignored the 1964 OAS sanctions by reestablishing relations with Cuba; finally, in 1975, the sanctions were relaxed. In the United States, the obvious failure of the 1960s policy of isolation and destabilization set in motion a slow but clear process of normalizing relations. Portions of the economic embargo were lifted, an anti-hijacking treaty was signed, and in 1974 secret negotiations on normalization were begun.[8]

During this period Cuba pursued a conciliatory foreign policy which reinforced these developments. Cuban policy toward Latin America was still aimed at breaking the island's diplomatic and economic isolation in the hemisphere, but the new climate of detente made conciliation a more viable strategy than revolution. With the U.S. threat sharply reduced, Cuba began to seriously pursue normalization of relations in hopes of establishing trade relations which would reduce its economic dependence on the USSR.[9]

The sharpest change in Cuba's foreign policy came in its relations with the rest of the Third World. With the security of the revolution virtually assured, Cuba was able to pursue much more vigorously a policy objective which during the 1960s had been of low priority relative to the aim of ensuring the revolution's survival. This objective was the expansion of Cuban influence in the Third World; it was pursued by an expansion of Cuban aid missions, a more vocal Cuban role in the Movement of Nonaligned Nations, and (eventually) by the deployment of Cuban combat troops in Africa.

II

CUBAN POLICY IN AFRICA, 1959-1975

Effectively isolated in the Western Hemisphere during the 1960s by the OAS, Cuba sought to expand its diplomatic and economic relations to other areas of the world. From the beginning, Cuba was drawn not only to the socialist camp, but also to progressive governments in the Third World—governments whose revolutionary experience paralleled Cuba's. In Africa, Cuba quickly developed very close relations with two such governments: Kwame Nkrumah's Ghana and Ben Bella's Algeria. The first Cuban military mission in Africa was established in Ghana in 1961; it was maintained until Nkrumah's ouster in 1966.[1] As early as 1960, Cuba provided military and medical supplies to the Algerian National Liberation Front (FLN), and after Algeria gained its independence in 1962, a Cuban military mission was established there which remained until the overthrow of Ben Bella in 1965. When the Algerian-Moroccan border war erupted in 1963, Cuba came to Algeria's aid with both arms and a battalion of combat troops—the first deployment of regular Cuban troops abroad.

The principal point of reference in the history of Cuba's involvement in Africa is Ernesto "Che" Guevara's extended tour of the continent in 1964-1965. Guevara visited virtually every "progressive" country on the continent—i.e., all those which had comprised the Casablanca Group prior to the inauguration of the Organization of African Unity: Algeria, Ghana, Guinea, Mali, and the United Arab Republic. He stopped in Algiers three times—once to deliver a stinging attack on Soviet trade policy to the Afro-Asian Peoples' Solidarity Organization.[2] His overall objective on this trip was to counter the USSR's withdrawal from involvement in sub-Saharan Africa by enlisting Ben Bella's support for the formation of a union of Third World nations. Led by Cuba and Algeria, this union would be aimed at combating imperialism and colonialism first in the Congo (Leopoldville) and then throughout all of Africa.[3]

In Congo-Brazzaville in 1964, Guevara met with leaders of the major nationalist movements in the Portuguese colonies. Within a

9

year Cuba began providing arms and instructions for the Movimiento Popular de Libertação de Angola (MPLA), the Partido Africano da Independencia da Guiné e Cabo Verde (PAIGC), and the Frente de Libertação de Mozambique (FRELIMO).

Though the effort to build a Third World anti-imperialist front came to naught, Guevara did not abandon his vision of African revolution. In April 1965, after resigning his Cuban citizenship and all his posts in the revolutionary government, Guevara arrived in Congo-Brazzaville to lead a force of two hundred Cuban "international fighters" against the Congolese regime of Moise Tshombe. From September to December, the Cubans fought alongside the Congolese guerrillas, but when Joseph Mobutu's coup overthrew Tshombe in November 1965, the Cubans' Congolese allies requested their departure so that they could arrange an armistice with the new regime. Guevara proceeded to Bolivia, but most of his troops stayed on in Africa, forming military missions to advise the governments of Congo-Brazzaville and Guinea and to train MPLA and PAIGC guerrillas.[4]

In 1965 and 1966, Cuba's two closest friends in Africa—Ben Bella and Nkrumah—were both deposed by coups d'etat. By demonstrating the vulnerability of progressive governments to military coup, these events prompted a new departure in Cuba's African policy. Cuba began providing fairly large military missions to friendly governments—missions intended not only to provide military training, but also to act as palace guards protecting those governments from their own military institutions.[5] In Congo-Brazzaville the Cuban force reached a peak of about one thousand in early 1966. It served as a presidential guard for Alphonse Massemba-Debat while at the same time training a militia—the Civil Defense Corps—to act as a politico-military counterweight to the Congolese army. In June 1966 the Cubans and the Cuban-trained militia thwarted an attempted coup. Nevertheless, Massemba-Debat, under domestic political pressure, gradually reduced the Cuban force to about 250 men over the next two years. When he was deposed in August 1968 by Marien Ngouabi, the Cuban mission was withdrawn except for the instructors at MPLA training camps on the Cabinda border. A similar Cuban mission was established in Guinea in 1966 at the request of President Sékou Touré, and continued throughout the 1970s. In November 1970 the Cubans played a key role in defeating a mercenary invasion of Guinea.[6]

Though Cuba's presence in Africa during the 1960s was modest, the basic direction of Cuban policy emerged quite clearly. Its overall objectives were to promote national liberation movements (by providing them with Cuban arms and advisors) and to help defend existing progressive movements (by furnishing Cuban military missions). When no backers were found for Guevara's proposal for a Third World anti-imperialist front, Cuba pursued its policy objectives unilaterally.

Cuban policy toward Africa was internationalist in that its motivation was essentially ideological. Cuba had little to gain economically or strategically by promoting revolution in Africa. Ideologically, however, Cuba has always taken the principle of international solidarity very seriously—no doubt because the survival of the Cuban revolution itself has been so dependent upon international assistance. Thus Cuban activism in Africa was motivated not by hopes of direct tangible benefits for Cuba, but rather in hopes of advancing the cause of socialism and establishing the principle of proletarian internationalism as a key ingredient of the foreign policies of *all* socialist countries. During the 1960s Cuba provided assistance to guerrillas in Senegal, Malawi, Mali, and Eritrea as well as to the nationalist movements in the Portuguese colonies.[7]

Ironically, Soviet policy toward Africa in the late 1960s was undergoing a transformation in precisely the opposite direction. In the late 1950s and early 1960s, Soviet African policy had also had a strong ideological component. Military and economic assistance was channeled to "revolutionary democrats" who showed evidence of pursuing progressive domestic and foreign policies (e.g., Guinea, Ghana, Mali, Morocco, UAR, Algeria), but the fall of Ben Bella and Nkrumah, coming in the wake of the defeat of the Soviet-supported rebellion in the Congo in 1964, shattered this policy. After 1966 the Soviets saw little prospect of any true revolutionary transformations in Africa, and Soviet policy was reformulated around geopolitical rather than ideological considerations. Soviet efforts were concentrated on areas of "inherent significance"—especially the area along the USSR's southern border (Iran, Turkey, India). Economic relations were oriented away from trying to use aid to gain political influence and toward relations that were directly beneficial to the Soviet Union. (This trade policy was decried by Guevara in 1965 as nearly indistinguishable from the policies of capitalist countries.)[8] Not surprisingly, this reorientation of Soviet policy meant a downgrading of relations with sub-Saharan Africa since the region had little inherent geopolitical significance. A comparison of Soviet aid to sub-Saharan Africa before and after 1966 shows a sharp decline in military and economic assistance.[9]

Obviously, Cuban policy in Africa during the 1960s was not being directed by or even coordinated with the USSR. As Cuban involvement was growing, based on a faith in the revolutionary potential of the continent, the Soviets' interest was waning precisely because they had lost that faith. Cuban and Soviet policies were not in conflict, but neither were they identical.

From 1968 to 1972 Cuba's foreign policy was in a quiescent period as the nation concentrated its energies on, first, the drive to produce 10 million tons of sugar in 1970 and, second, economic recovery from the failure of that drive. The reemergence of Cuba on the world scene in 1972 was punctuated by a two-month tour by Fidel Castro of Africa, Eastern Europe, and the Soviet Union. Shortly thereafter, Cuban military missions of approximately one hundred advisors were dispatched to Sierra Leone and Equatorial Guinea while smaller technical missions were sent to Somalia in 1974, Algeria in 1975, and Tanzania.[10]

Cuba's major military commitments in the early 1970s were in the Middle East rather than in Africa. Several hundred Cuban advisors arrived in South Yemen in early 1973 to train both the People's Democratic Republic of Yemen's army and Dhofari guerrillas fighting in Oman.* When Iran intervened in the Dhofari rebellion, the Cuban presence in Yemen was escalated rapidly to 600-700 men. Then, when war broke out in 1973 between Israel and the Arab states, Cuba sent 500-750 armored troops to aid Syria[11]—only the second time Cuba had committed regular combat troops abroad. The policy guidelines were unchanged since the first such commitment (Algeria, 1963): a friendly progressive state was faced with a serious external threat to its security. This same decision-rule, as we shall see, continued to govern Cuba's deployment of combat troops abroad throughout the 1970s.

---

*Begun in the late 1960s, the Dhofari guerrilla movement sought to replace the conservative government in Oman with a radical Marxist one. The Dhofaris received aid from Iraq and South Yemen until their defeat in 1975 by an Iranian expeditionary force.

III

CUBAN INVOLVEMENT IN ANGOLA, 1965-1979

A. CUBAN RELATIONS WITH THE MPLA, 1965-1974

Cuba's first contact with the MPLA came in the early 1960s, and its military assistance program to the MPLA dates from 1965. Che Guevara conferred with MPLA President Agostinho Neto in Congo-Brazzaville during Guevara's 1965 diplomatic tour; later that year, when Guevara's guerrilla force withdrew from its abortive effort to overthrow Tshombe's government in Congo-Leopoldville (hereafter Zaire), part of it remained in Congo-Brazzaville to establish training camps for the MPLA.[1]

From this point onward, Cuban support for the MPLA was uninterrupted. The MPLA participated as the Angolan delegation to the Tri-Continental Conference held in Havana in 1966, and President Neto along with MPLA military commander Endo visited Cuba that same year. Shortly thereafter, MPLA students and guerrilla recruits began arriving in Cuba for education and military training.[2] The level of Cuban assistance to the MPLA appears to have remained relatively constant from its initiation in 1966 until 1975; it consisted of arms and training programs both within Cuba and in Congo-Brazzaville.

Cuba's early preference for the MPLA over its rivals—Holden Roberto's Frente Nacional de Libertação de Angola (FNLA) and later Jonas Savimbi's União Nacional para a Independência Total de Angola (UNITA)—was primarily ideological. Not only was the MPLA the oldest liberation movement in Angola, but it was also by far the most ideologically sophisticated; founded in 1956, it appears to have been directly descended from the merger of the Angolan Communist Party with several radical nationalist groups. From the outset the MPLA has adhered to a staunchly anti-imperialist, multiracialist, and pro-socialist ideological position, and it has pursued a strategy of political organization primarily among the mestiço and black urban working class of Luanda.[3]

In contrast the FNLA, which is descended from the União das Populações de Angola (UPA), began as a rural, tribally based separatist movement of the Bakongo people in northern Angola. Though it abandoned its separatist aspirations in 1958, the FNLA never escaped an essentially tribalist orientation. To the extent that the FNLA exhibited an ideology, it was a rudimentary appeal to racialism (anti-white, anti-mestiço, tribalist, and anti-Communist). Not surprisingly, the FNLA's strategy for ending Portuguese rule varied sharply from the MPLA's. While the MPLA emphasized political education and mobilization, the FNLA's approach was essentially military.[4] Moreover, Roberto refused to cooperate with the MPLA in any sort of unified front, going so far as to execute MPLA guerrillas who attempted to set up operations in northern Angola. From the late 1960s on, fighting between the two groups was endemic.[5]

Founded in 1966 by Savimbi, a former FNLA member, UNITA was also based predominantly upon a tribal group—the Ovimbundu peoples in the rural south. Though Savimbi initially propounded a Maoist theory of self-reliance, he has proven adept at shifting ideological ground in pursuit of outside aid. During the late 1960s and early 1970s UNITA fought more against the MPLA than against the Portuguese, with whom it at times had a working relationship of peaceful coexistence.[6] Like the FNLA, UNITA relied mainly upon a primitive ideological mixture of racialism and tribal populism.[7]

The Cubans had more than ideological reasons for believing that an MPLA government would be a good deal more progressive than one dominated by either of its rivals. The MPLA drew almost all of its foreign support from the socialist bloc and from the former members of the progressive Casablanca Group within the OAU—the countries with which Cuba felt the closest kinship (and which Guevara had visited in 1964-65). Both Nkrumah and Ben Bella were vocal supporters of the MPLA. Finally, as a member of the Conferência das Organizações Nationalistas das Colónias Portuguesas (CONCP), the MPLA benefitted from its association with the two strongest members—FRELIMO and the PAIGC—both of which received Cuban assistance.[8]

The FNLA, on the other hand, received almost all of its aid from pro-Western Zaire. After the assassination of Patrice Lumumba in 1961, Cuba regarded the succession of Zairean governments as all more or less reactionary puppets of imperialism. The Cubans accused both Roberto and his patron Mobutu of having CIA connections long before it became publicly known that Roberto had been put on a CIA retainer in 1962.[9] Cuba also accused Mobutu of hiring Cuban exiles to train FNLA recruits in Zaire.[10] In contrast to the FNLA, UNITA received only meager outside aid during the 1960s, but Savimbi travelled with a black anti-Castro Cuban—

14

Carlos More—who had campaigned in Africa against the "racism" of the Cuban revolution.[11]

It is hardly surprising, then, that Cuba chose to aid the progressive, anti-imperialist MPLA over the pro-Western, anti-Communist FNLA and UNITA. No doubt these same reasons had led the Soviet Union to begin aiding the MPLA several years earlier. Yet while Soviet policy toward Africa in the mid-1960s was shifting away from an ideological and toward a more geopolitical orientation, ideological considerations remained paramount for Cuba. In the case of Angola, this difference in perspective led to differences in practical policy.

While Cuban aid to the MPLA was consistent and uninterrupted, Soviet aid was halted twice—once in 1963-64 (before Cuban aid began) and again in 1972. The first interruption in Soviet support followed a diplomatic debacle suffered by the MPLA in the OAU in October 1963: the OAU's African Liberation Committee granted recognition to the FNLA's Revolutionary Government of Angola in Exile, largely because of the MPLA's military weakness. A year later the OAU adopted a new position favoring unity between the FNLA and MPLA (thus granting the MPLA tacit if not official recognition), and Soviet aid resumed.[12]

This first interruption of Soviet aid might be interpreted as the USSR abiding by the OAU's 1963 decision, but the second cannot. In 1972-73 the Portuguese army launched a series of major offensives in Angola which resulted in severe military setbacks for the MPLA. These defeats exacerbated political divisions within the movement, leading to a number of defections. In 1973, MPLA military commanders in the Mbunda area west of Zambia formed the "Eastern Rebellion Group" under the leadership of Daniel Chipenda and broke away from the MPLA to later join the FNLA. In 1974 another group of dissidents unhappy with Neto's leadership also left the movement and formed the "Active Rebellion Group."[13] With the MPLA in military retreat and political disarray, Soviet aid began to decline in 1972 and by early 1974 had been halted altogether. The Soviets apparently found Neto a difficult person to deal with, and for a brief period courted favor with Chipenda.[14]

B. THE ANGOLAN CIVIL WAR, 1974-1976

When the Portuguese Armed Forces Movement overthrew the Caetano regime in April 1974, Soviet and Cuban policies in Africa

15

were not only operating under different assumptions, but in the case of Angola were at odds (though not belligerently so). Two developments during the summer of 1974 brought Cuban and Soviet policies toward Angola into harmony. The first was the arrival in June of Chinese arms and military instructors for the FNLA; the second was a decision by the United States in July to begin shipping arms to the FNLA through Zaire.[15] In November, just six months after it had been cut off, Soviet aid to the MPLA resumed. (There is no evidence of any significant increase in either Soviet or Cuban aid over the levels established in the late 1960s.)

Some commentators have suggested that the expanded Chinese involvement in Angola was the principal motivation for the Soviet response.[16] There is no doubt that the Sino-Soviet rivalry for influence in the Third World has been a major concern of Soviet policymakers and that southern Africa had proven to be a fertile area for Chinese initiatives. During the late 1960s and early 1970s, while the Soviet intervention in Czechoslovakia was still fresh in the minds of many Africans, China successfully established links with Zambia, Tanzania, FRELIMO in Mozambique, and the Zimbabwe African National Union (ZANU) in Zimbabwe. The prospect of a pro-Chinese Angola must have been all the more anathema to the Soviets in the light of such circumstances, while the coincidence (the Soviets suspected coordination) of U.S. and Chinese aid to the FNLA raised the specter of a U.S.-Chinese alliance against the USSR.[17] To allow such a venture to succeed would only encourage its repetition.

Under OAU pressure, Neto, Roberto, and Savimbi met in Portugal in January 1975 to negotiate a peaceful transition to independence. The resulting Alvor Agreements established a tripartite transitional government, called for a single national army, and set November 11, 1975 as the date for Angolan independence.[18] The uneasy peace established at Alvor was short-lived as the conflict between the three liberation movements rapidly became internationalized.

Immediately after Alvor, the U.S. "40 Committee"* authorized (at the urging of the CIA) an increase in covert aid to the FNLA. Given the FNLA's long commitment to a military solution in Angola, its military superiority, and its history of opposition to cooperation with the MPLA, such an increase in U.S. aid could only have had the effect of undermining the FNLA's adherence to the Alvor

*A crisis-management committee of the senior policymakers charged with overseeing covert operations.

Agreements. Indeed, in March 1975, bolstered by new shipments of U.S. arms, the FNLA launched an attack on MPLA offfices in Luanda and expelled the MPLA from the northern territories under FNLA control. Later that month, the conflict was further internationalized when 1,200 regular troops from Zaire entered Angola to fight alongside the FNLA. These reinforcements gave the combined forces of the FNLA/Zaire and UNITA a four-to-one advantage over the MPLA.[19]

The MPLA responded to this escalation of fighting by seeking additional aid from both the USSR and Cuba. The Soviets quickly stepped up their flow of arms, and after a meeting between Neto and Cuban Comandante Flavio Bravo in May, Cuba agreed to provide several hundred instructors to open four military training camps for MPLA recruits. According to most accounts, 230 Cuban instructors arrived in Angola in June.[20]

The fighting between the MPLA and the FNLA/Zaire-UNITA coalition abated in June during an abortive attempt to revive the Alvor Agreements, but intensified again in early July. After expelling FNLA troops from Luanda, the MPLA launched a campaign to gain control of Angola's provincial capitals before November 11; by mid-July the MPLA's political strength in urban areas had helped it achieve significant military successes despite being outnumbered by its opponents in the FNLA/Zaire-UNITA coalition. It appeared that November 11 would bring an independent Angola with an MPLA government.

The precarious position of the pro-Western forces in July catalyzed a new escalation of international intervention. Both the FNLA and UNITA turned to South Africa for assistance, while their backers—Zaire and Zambia—appealed to the United States. Both the United States and South Africa responded positively in at least partial conjunction with one another.[21] On July 17 the U.S. "40 Committee" authorized a massive expansion of arms aid to both the FNLA and UNITA, as well as a program of covert action by the CIA. "Operation Feature," as the covert program was called, included the recruitment of mercenaries, the use of CIA personnel as military advisors in both Zaire and northern Angola, and $32 million in armaments (worth approximately $65 million after adjusting for the normal undervaluation of such stocks).[22] On July 20—only three days after the "40 Committee" decision—the FNLA, joined by right-wing Portuguese military and secret police, launched an offensive aimed at capturing Luanda before November 11. As fighting in the north intensified, South African troops crossed the Namibian border on August 9 and took up positions a few miles inside Angola at the Cunene River hydroelectric project. Shortly thereafter, South Africa opened training bases for both the FNLA and UNITA in Namibia and southern Angola.[23]

These escalations once again led the MPLA to ask its allies for additional aid, including military advisors. An MPLA delegation to Moscow in August found the Soviets unwilling to provide more than arms, but the Cubans proved to be more responsive.[24] A military delegation headed by Raúl Díaz Arguelles* visited Luanda in late August, and several hundred additional Cuban troops left for Angola shortly thereafter.[25]

At this point, Cuban-Soviet coordination in Angola was still relatively limited. Each country continued to follow its historic policy of aiding the MPLA, and the level of aid provided by each had been growing gradually since early 1975. The policies of both were essentially reactive: each increase in aid came at the request of the MPLA in response to escalations by the MPLA's opponents— domestic and foreign. Through the summer of 1975 Cuba and the USSR appeared to be making independent decisions about their aid to the MPLA; as the compatibility of these decisions became clear, greater coordination was established. This reconstruction of developments is indirectly supported by John Marcum, who notes that early Cuban arrivals brought their own heavy weapons. With the increases in Soviet arms shipments, this became unnecessary, and in later stages of the civil war, Cuban troops brought only light arms; heavier weapons were sent directly from the USSR, and were waiting for the Cubans when they arrived.[26]

Fighting in Angola was intense throughout September and early October 1975, but the MPLA with its Cuban advisors and Soviet arms was holding its own against FNLA and Zairean troops in the north. In the south, UNITA was no match for the strengthened MPLA. With independence only weeks away, it appeared unlikely that the MPLA could be dislodged from Luanda before the Portuguese departure.

Probably as a consequence of its allies' inability to gain the upper hand on the battlefield, South Africa intervened directly in the Angolan civil war on October 23. Under the code name "Operation Zulu," some five thousand South African troops launched an armored assault from Namibia. The Chipenda Column, as the force was called, moved rapidly up the coast, covering five hundred

*Diaz later became commander of the Cuban forces in Angola and was killed in combat against the South Africans.

18

kilometers in just over a week. Faced with a suddenly desperate military situation, the MPLA on November 4 asked for Cuban troops to help defend Luanda; on November 5, Cuba agreed. One battalion was airlifted immediately to Angola with the objective of holding Luanda until reinforcements could arrive. This first combat unit landed on November 8 as additional troops left Cuba by sea.[27]

Militarily, Cuba's troops made the difference. From November 1975 to March 1976, between 18,000 and 36,000 Cubans arrived in Angola (see Table 1). By mid-December the South African advance in the south had been halted, and the MPLA-Cuban forces had gone over to the offensive against the FNLA-Zairean forces on the northern front. When the U.S. Congress prohibited further U.S. aid to the FNLA or UNITA, South Africa withdrew its troops to the border, charging that the United States had defaulted on its pledge to provide whatever military assistance was required to defeat the MPLA. Without the South Africans, UNITA quickly disintegrated as a fighting force. By early February, Cuba and the MPLA were able to concentrate their forces in the north, and within a few weeks the FNLA was in full retreat across the border, seeking refuge in Zaire. The collapse of UNITA and the FNLA was so rapid that by mid-March Castro and Neto were able to agree to a schedule for Cuban troop withdrawals.

Diplomatically, South Africa's troops made the difference. Any residual African support for the MPLA's opponents or for a negotiated settlement of the war was quickly erased by the South African intervention. On January 22 the OAU condemned South Africa while pointedly refusing to condemn Cuba or the USSR. On February 11 it admitted the People's Republic of Angola (PRA) to membership, thereby recognizing the legitimacy of the MPLA government. Nigeria is an instructive example in this regard. Nigeria recognized the PRA on November 27 and began sending it aid, even though the MPLA's military position was still highly tenuous. One of the most important and most consistently pro-Western countries of sub-Saharan Africa, Nigeria explicitly praised Cuban and Soviet aid to the PRA in its struggle to defeat South African intervention. The U.S. Congressional cutoff of aid to the FNLA and UNITA, which led directly to South Africa's withdrawal, resulted at least in part from the Congress's unwillingness to associate U.S. policy in Africa so closely with the South Africans. Deprived of U.S. and South African support, the FNLA and UNITA were no match whatsoever for the combined MPLA-Cuban forces.

CUBA'S POLICY IN AFRICA, 1959-1980

Table 1

NUMBER OF CUBAN TROOPS AND MILITARY ADVISORS IN ANGOLA,
1975-1980

Year/Month	Estimates Based on Western Intelligence	Estimates Based on Cuban or MPLA Sources
1975		
June	230	230
October	1000-1500	480
November	3000	2800
December	5000[a]	—
1976		
January	9000[b]	--
March	15,000-18,000[c]	36,000
November	12,000-13,000[d]	—
1977		
February	—	12,000
November	19,000[e]	—
1978	18,000-20,000	—
1979	18,000-20,000	—

Sources: For Western intelligence estimates: John Marcum, *The Angolan Revolution* (Cambridge: MIT Press, 1978), pp. 271ff.; William J. Durch, *The Cuban Military in Africa and the Middle East* (Arlington, Va.: Center for Naval Analysis, 1977), pp. 44ff.; *Washington Post*, December 11, 1975; January 17, 1976; November 15, 1977; September 14, 1979; *New York Times*, December 12, 1975. For Cuban or MPLA estimates: Gabriel García-Marquez, "Operation Carlota," *New Left Review* 101-102 (February-April 1977); Barry A. Sklar, *Cuba: Normalization of Relations* (Congressional Research Service Issue Brief No. IB75030; Washington, D.C.: Library of Congress, 1977); *International Bulletin*, June 4, 1976; *New York Times*, January 12, 1976; December 7, 1977; February 8, 1980.

[a]Estimate for mid-December. (Cuban troops were arriving in December at an estimated rate of 400 per week.)

[b]Estimate for mid-January. (Cuban troops were arriving in January at an estimated rate of 1000 per week.)

[c]Estimate of peak strength in 1976. (Cuban troop arrivals fell off in late February and early March.)

[d]Low point after Cuban withdrawals.

[e]High point after reinforcements; constant since then.

It is almost certain that Cuba's decision to commit large numbers of troops in regular combat units was an independent one—not one directed by the Soviet Union. Though it represented a qualitative escalation of Cuban military assistance, it was nevertheless in line with Cuba's decade-long policy toward Angola. Moreover, it was also wholly consistent with Cuba's well-established policy of giving military aid to progressive African liberation movements generally—a policy which arose in the mid-1960s not from Soviet urging but at a time when Cuba perceived a weakening of Soviet willingness to live up to the principles of proletarian internationalism. In addition, Cuba's intervention in Angola fit the basic criterion Cuban policymakers had apparently employed in making previous commitments of regular troops in Algeria (1963) and Syria (1973): the MPLA was a friendly progressive movement (in Cuba's view, the only legitimate claimant to govern Angola) beset by direct imperialist intervention which threatened its survival.

Cuba has denied from the outset that the decision to intervene in Angola was taken at Soviet behest. In his major discussion of Angola on April 19, 1976, Fidel Castro described the Cuban-Soviet relationship as follows:

> Cuba made its decision completely on its own responsibility. The USSR, which had always helped the peoples of the Portuguese colonies in the struggle for their independence and provided besieged Angola with basic aid in military equipment and collaborated with our efforts when imperialism had cut off practically all our air routes to Africa, never requested that a single Cuban be sent to that country. The USSR is extraordinarily respectful and careful in its relations with Cuba. A decision of that nature could only be made by our own party.[28]

Gabriel García-Marquez, in his quasi-official account of Cuba's role in Angola, goes so far as to say that the Soviet Union was not even consulted until the decision to intervene had been made. Soviet sources have confirmed that the Cuban decision was an independent one, and in early 1976 even Secretary of State Henry Kissinger voiced his opinion to that effect.[29] Indeed the USSR was probably hesitant to make a major commitment in Angola for fear of provoking a confrontation with the West in an area of low strategic priority for the Soviets—a confrontation which might well have had reverberations in policy areas of much greater strategic importance (e.g., detente, strategic arms limitation, and Sino-Western relations). In any event, the Soviet involvement proceeded much more cautiously than the Cuban involvement. In August 1975 the USSR refused the MPLA's request for military advisors, and though several hundred were finally dispatched to Luanda in November, the Soviet role remained primarily that of arms supplier.[30] It was the Cubans who, along with MPLA commanders, planned the conduct of the war. Even Soviet logistical support for the Cuban intervention seems to have had its limits. Though the rapid deployment of Cuban troops in November was critical for the MPLA's survival, the Cubans came to Angola by means of converted freighters and obsolete commercial airplanes. The USSR's willingness to provide air transport for the Cubans was very equivocal. The Soviets flew Cuban troops to the staging areas in Congo-Brazzaville during early December, but suspended the flights after a U.S. protest. The flights resumed after the U.S. Congress prohibited U.S. involvement in the war, but stopped again after a second U.S. protest. They resumed once more in January 1976, and continued for several weeks after U.S. diplomatic pressure had successfully denied the Cuban planes landing rights in several countries, making the continued use of Cuban commercial air transport impossible.[31]

The evidence indicates that, through the summer of 1975, Cuba and the USSR decided independently to expand their assistance programs to the MPLA as the civil war became increasingly internationalized. As the compatibility of their policies became clear, the Cubans and Soviets began coordinating their actions. They did *not* hatch a plot to intervene in Angola as an opening move in a joint offensive against Western influence in Africa. On the contrary, increases in Cuban and Soviet aid were essentially reactive. The West, especially the United States, initiated the internationalization of the Angolan conflict by escalating its aid to the FNLA in hopes of promoting a military solution that would deprive the MPLA of any effective role in the coalition government outlined at Alvor. In view of both Cuba's and the USSR's history of support for the MPLA, U.S. actions virtually guaranteed a concomitant increase in Cuban and Soviet involvement, thus transforming the local conflict into an East-West confrontation. Indeed U.S. intelligence analysts predicted as much.[32] The most grievous failing of U.S. policy was that the United States provoked such a confrontation in a situation where, due to the weakness of its local allies and its inevitable association with South Africa, it could not possibly win.

C. CUBAN ASSISTANCE TO THE PRA SINCE 1976

The Cuban troop buildup in Angola slowed in late February 1976 as the FNLA and UNITA disintegrated. Two weeks later, Castro and Neto met and agreed to a gradual withdrawal of Cuban troops at the rate of two hundred per week, though Cuba pledged to continue providing the "military units and weapons necessary to support the People's Republic of Angola in case of aggression from the outside."[33] Cuban withdrawals continued throughout 1976, with the Cuban force reaching a low point of about twelve thousand in early 1977.

As Cuban troops departed, civilian advisors of all sorts streamed into Angola. In July 1976 Cuba and the PRA concluded a series of economic and technical agreements providing for Cuban teachers, engineers, medical personnel, and construction workers to help build Angola's new socialist society. Over the next year and a half, approximately 2,600 Cuban technicians went to Angola; a new series of accords signed in November 1977 resulted in a doubling of that figure during 1978.[34] Such assistance was particularly crucial for the PRA since the combined effects of Portuguese colonialism and the civil war had left the nation devastated.

Though Cuba's military presence in Angola declined during 1976, the PRA's security was by no means assured. UNITA guerrillas continued operating in south-central Angola with South African support, and the South Africans conducted repeated raids into Angola to strike at guerrilla camps of the South West African People's Organization (SWAPO). Though Zaire had recognized the PRA in March 1976, armed conflicts on the Zairean border were common, and Zaire continued its aid to the remnants of the FNLA and to the secessionist Front pour la Libération de l'Enclave de Cabinda (FLEC). These circumstances alone would probably have slowed or halted the Cuban withdrawal eventually, but two events in early 1977 led to a reversal of the withdrawal policy and a reinforcement of the Cuban presence.

The first occurred in March, when several thousand Katangan gendarmes invaded Zaire's Shaba province (formerly Katanga) from western Angola.[35] Organized by mercenaries in 1960 and supported by the West, the Katangans had fought for an independent Katanga under Moise Tshombe during the Congolese civil war. Many went into exile in Angola in 1963 after being put down by the UN intervention force; others followed after Mobutu's 1975 coup. During the late 1960s the Katangans fought with the Portuguese against Angola's nationalists, but during the civil war they sided with the MPLA. As a consequence they had been the recipients of both arms and military training from the Cubans.

Zaire immediately charged that Angola and Cuba had staged the Shaba invasion and that Cubans were advising the rebels. Cuba denied any involvement. Indeed the invasion was particularly ill-timed from the Cuban point of view: it occurred right in the middle of a major Cuban diplomatic initiative in Africa. At the beginning of March, Fidel Castro set out on his most extensive foreign tour since 1972, visiting Algeria, Libya, Somalia, Ethiopia, South Yemen, Tanzania, Mozambique, Angola, the USSR, and the German Democratic Republic. While the fighting was still raging in Shaba, Castro held a press conference in Dar es Salaam during which he stated categorically that there was "not a single Cuban" in Zaire, and that Cuba had neither trained nor armed the Katangans for the invasion. Mobutu's claim of Cuban involvement, Castro charged, was simply a ploy to obtain Western aid for his tottering regime.[36]

The U.S. response to Shaba was surprisingly mild. Both Secretary of State Cyrus Vance and President Carter acknowledged that there was no evidence of Cuban involvement in the invasion.[37] Though they absolved the Cubans of complicity, the Western nations were deeply concerned about the stability of Zaire. Weakened by corruption and deeply in debt, Mobutu's regime appeared seriously imperiled by the Katangans. By all accounts the Katangan force was warmly received by the population of Shaba, and the invasion sparked rebellions in several other southern provinces. The loss of Shaba would mean the loss of Zaire's principal source of foreign exchange (copper from the mines at Kolwezi), the loss of substantial Belgian and French foreign investments, and near certain bankruptcy for Zaire. Egypt, Sudan, West Germany, Saudi Arabia, Morocco, France, Belgium, China, and the United States all came to Mobutu's aid. Some 1,500 Moroccan troops with French and Belgian advisors were flown in to bolster the ineffectual Zairean army, and by late April the Katangans were in retreat across the Angolan border.

It is exceedingly unlikely that the Cubans would have staged or even encouraged such a provocative action by the Katangans in the middle of Castro's African tour. For both Cuba and Angola the invasion sharply increased the threat of war with Zaire, and a wide array of Western countries were obviously ready to come to Zaire's aid in such an eventuality. By aggravating Angola's security problems, the invasion undermined Cuba's policy of troop withdrawals. Lacking evidence to the contrary, Cuba's denials of involvement can probably be taken at face value. Angola's role in the invasion is less clear. Part of the March 1976 recognition agreement between Zaire and Angola provided for Angola to restrain the Katangans in exchange for Zaire ending its support of the FNLA. Not only did Zaire fail to keep this bargain, but during the early months of 1977 there was a sharp increase in Zairean border incursions into Angola. A number of commentators have suggested that the PRA retaliated by giving the Katangans the go-ahead to invade Shaba.[38] If this is in fact what happened, it demonstrates that Neto and the MPLA were not above making decisions that might damage Cuba's wider foreign policy interests despite the close relationship between Cuba and the PRA. Perhaps this was the sort of behavior that had made the Soviets wary of Neto in the past.

The second event in early 1977 which precipitated the reversal of Cuba's withdrawal policy was a challenge to Neto's leadership from within the MPLA—a challenge backed by the USSR. (Soviet distrust of Neto had remained much the same since their falling out in 1972.) In May 1977 a faction of the MPLA led by Nito Alves staged a coup attempt in Luanda. The differences between Neto and Nito Alves went back at least as far as 1972, but after the civil war Alves and his supporters began a systematic attempt to gain control of strategic posts in the PRA's emerging political structure with the eventual goal of unseating Neto. Ideologically, Alves opposed Neto's position of nonalignment, his policy of gradual transition to socialism, and his firm support of multiracialism. Alves's "fractionalists," as they came to be called, favored alignment with the USSR, a more rapid pace of social transformation, and a black nationalist stance on the race issue.[39] The attempted coup had at least the tacit support of the USSR, which knew of it in advance but did nothing to warn Neto. The coup-makers did not inform the Cubans, however, and when the coup attempt took place, Cuban troops joined with MPLA forces loyal to Neto to suppress it.[40] While the MPLA has never publicly accused the Soviet Union of complicity in the coup attempt, relations between the PRA and USSR cooled considerably in 1977 and 1978, while Angola's relations with Cuba continued to be very friendly.[41]

Confronted with the multiple problems of guerrilla resistance from UNITA, a threat of war with Zaire over Shaba, the persistent danger of South African intervention, and its own internal divisions, the MPLA requested a reinforcement of the Cuban military presence early in 1977.[42] The Cuban decision to reverse its withdrawal policy was probably made in June when Raúl Castro visited Luanda. Over the ensuing months, the number of Cuban troops in Angola increased by some 20 percent to approximately nineteen thousand men. To date, withdrawals have not been resumed.

Despite these reinforcements, Angola's security situation deteriorated in early 1978. UNITA stepped up its guerrilla attacks, and the possibility of South African intervention appeared to increase.[43] On May 6, South African planes struck 155 miles inside Angola with an air raid on the Kassinga camp for Namibian refugees; over six hundred refugees were killed. Such deep raids were reminiscent of South Africa's maneuvers prior to the 1975 invasion, and the PRA anticipated a new intervention throughout 1978.[44]

The major threat to Angolan security in 1978, however, was "Shaba II." On May 11, the Katangans launched a virtual carbon copy of their 1977 attack on Shaba, but this time with greater success.[45] By May 13 they had captured Kolwezi. Once again the West came to Mobutu's aid. French and Belgian paratroopers dropped on Kolwezi from U.S. transport planes, and amidst charges and countercharges of massacres and atrocities, they recaptured the city. The Katangans retreated across the border into Angola as they had in 1977. Mobutu again charged the Cubans and Angolans with complicity in the invasion; again they denied it. Castro went so far as to summon the head of the U.S. Interests Section in Cuba, Lyle Lane, to give his personal assurance that Cuba was not behind the invasion. In fact, Castro told Lane, he had tried to prevent the invasion, but to no avail. Angola, Castro observed, needed peace above all, and the Katangans only aggravated Angola's international situation.[46]

Despite the obvious similarities between the two invasions, the U.S. reaction to Shaba II was distinctly different from its reaction to Shaba I a year earlier. In 1977 the United States had accepted Cuba's claims of noninvolvement, but in 1978 it directly accused Cuba of staging the invasion.[47] However, the intelligence reports on which this charge was purportedly based proved to be less than convincing to the State Department, the CIA, and both foreign affairs committees of the Congress—all of whom found the evidence of Cuban involvement to be inconclusive; only the White House interpreted them as decisive.[48] The U.S. accusation elicited sharp denials from Cuba, and a heated public debate between Carter and Castro ensued. The White House was eventually forced to retreat from its initial claim that Cuba plotted the invasion to the rather different position that Cuba could have done more to prevent it.[49]

The difference in the U.S. responses to Shaba I and Shaba II had little to do with either Angola or Shaba; it was based upon what was occurring across the continent in Ethiopia. In 1977 Cuba's presence in Angola was already a year old, and the number of Cuban troops was drawing down. The Carter administration had just come into office, bringing with it a clear intention to normalize U.S.-Cuban relations. It was inclined to accept Cuba's assurances that Angola was an exceptional case rather than a model for future interventions. In this atmosphere the Administration was predisposed to evaluate Shaba I in the best possible light. Shaba II, on the other hand, followed in the wake of the Cuban-Soviet intervention in Ethiopia—an event which sharply altered U.S. perceptions of Cuban and Soviet intentions in Africa. The circumstances of the Ethiopian conflict prevented any effective U.S. response, but Shaba II gave the Administration a convenient opportunity to vent its anger at Cuba's African policy in general, despite the paucity of evidence supporting the claims of Cuban involvement. The new U.S. "hardline" on Cuba exacerbated Cuban and Angolan fears of renewed foreign intervention against the PRA, further delaying any significant Cuban troop reduction. Their fears were fully justified: on May 24, Senator Dick Clark (D-Iowa), Chairman of the Senate Foreign Relations Subcommittee on African Affairs, revealed that the CIA was proposing a new assistance program for UNITA.[50] Because of the publicity the plan was apparently scuttled.

In mid-1978 Angola's security situation began improving somewhat. On June 28, Deputy U.S. Representative to the UN Donald McHenry traveled to Angola to seek SWAPO's acceptance of the UN plan for Namibian independence and to help negotiate a rapprochement between Angola and Zaire. Both efforts were successful, and two months later Neto met with Mobutu in Kinshasa to conclude an agreement. Zaire agreed to end its border incursions and to halt aid to UNITA, FLEC, and the FNLA; in return, Angola agreed to disarm the Katangans and to reopen the Benguela railroad to facilitate the shipment of Zaire's copper to the Atlantic coast for export. So far, this 1978 agreement has held up well, though Angola has been unable to keep the railroad open with any consistency.

These agreements to ensure peaceful transition in Namibia and to establish detente between Angola and Zaire are both very much in Angola's interest. Not only do they reduce the threat of direct conflict between the PRA and Zaire or South Africa, but they also mean an end to UNITA's principal sources of external aid. The two agreements are also valuable for the West. Since SWAPO is the only guerrilla organization operating in Namibia, a full-scale military struggle for independence there would inevitably result in a SWAPO government dependent on Cuba and the USSR for military supplies—and perhaps even troops. In Zaire, Mobutu's survival depends upon putting an end to the Katangan threat so that full-capacity copper production can be resumed. Otherwise, Zaire will almost certainly default on its mammoth external debt, and it is doubtful that Mobutu could weather such a crisis.[51]

If Cuban policy in Africa is (as the United States portrays it) aimed at stirring up conflicts to provide excuses for further intervention, then one would have expected Cuba to create obstacles to both the Namibian and PRA-Zairean agreements. Cuba's actual policy was quite the opposite. State Department officials concede that Cuba played a "positive role" in achieving these agreements. Along with the PRA, Cuba helped convince a reluctant SWAPO to accept the UN plan for Namibia, and Cuban troops helped to disarm the Katangans and then relocate them away from the Zairean border.[52] Cuba's objective in southern Africa thus far has not been to exacerbate conflicts, but rather to reduce those conflicts that threaten Angola's security. That, after all, is a precondition for Cuban troop withdrawals from the PRA.

A substantial reduction in the number of Cuban troops in Angola is unlikely in the near future. Though the accord between Angola and Zaire has held up well, the prospects for a peaceful transition to majority rule in Namibia are still uncertain at best. South African troops continue to strike at Angola's border territories, and UNITA guerrillas are still active with South African support. The death of Agostinho Neto in September 1979 may well aggravate the factional disputes within the MPLA, making it all the more difficult for the government to consolidate its internal security.[53]

D. THE COSTS AND BENEFITS OF INTERVENTION

The commitment of thousands of troops in Angola was such an unprecedented projection of Cuban military strength abroad that it posed risks Cuba had not encountered since the attempted installation of Soviet IRBMs in Cuba in 1962. In presenting the Cuban account of the Angolan decision, García-Marquez reports that Cuban policymakers weighed two major risks: (1) that the United States would respond militarily either in Angola or against Cuba directly, and (2) that Cuba's involvement might provoke a confrontation between the United States and the USSR, destroying detente and threatening international peace. Both of these contingencies were dismissed as unlikely, largely because of the domestic political climate in the United States. Having just extricated itself from Vietnam, the United States was not likely to have much stomach for a new foreign intervention. The executive branch, weakened by Watergate and headed by an unelected President, would probably be unable to sustain Congressional support for any major U.S. response. With the CIA under close scrutiny for its past abuses, even a covert U.S. response would probably be limited. Internationally, Soviet support for Cuba lessened the likelihood of a U.S. strike against Cuba itself, and U.S. hesitancy to openly ally with South Africa mitigated against a direct U.S. role in Angola.[54] If this is a faithful summary of the Cuban leadership's political calculus in 1975, it was very astute indeed. Cuba avoided the major dangers inherent in its intervention for precisely the reasons outlined.

An analysis of the costs and benefits to Cuba of the Angolan intervention shows that the benefits greatly exceeded the costs, and that it was fairly clear from the outset that this would be the case if the military operation proved successful. The greatest benefit, of course, was the establishment of a socialist Angola under MPLA control. Without Cuban intervention, it is almost certain that the MPLA would have been defeated militarily by the combined onslaught of FNLA, UNITA, Zairean, and South African troops. Defeat of the MPLA, with which Cuba had maintained close ties for a decade, would have meant a pro-Western government in Luanda and hence a setback for the liberation movements in both Namibia and Zimbabwe. The MPLA's victory, however, significantly advanced both these struggles by adding a militant new member to the "Front Line" states. For SWAPO in particular, it meant a friendly rear base and source of supply just across the Namibian border. Thus, both directly and indirectly, Cuban intervention advanced the cause of national liberation in southern Africa—the keystone of Cuba's African policy since the mid-1960s.

Diplomatically, the intervention was unlikely to damage Cuban relations with the rest of Africa since it was directed against the South Africans. (As noted earlier, Nigeria is the paradigm case of a pro-Western nation that approved Cuba's involvement because of South Africa's intervention.) Cuban prestige was actually enhanced by the intervention. It demonstrated that Cuba was willing to commit the lives and blood of its people to the anti-imperialist struggle in Africa without asking either military or economic concessions in return. Cuba was the Third World's David defeating the South African Goliath.

In Latin America, memories of Cuban aid to guerrillas in the late 1960s outweighed animosity to white minority rule in southern Africa; thus Cuban troops in Angola revived fears of Cuban hemispheric intervention. However, though some of the moderate Latin American governments (e.g., Venezuela, Colombia) voiced disapproval of Cuba's actions, they refused to halt the process of normalizing relations with Cuba, despite U.S. prompting toward that end.[55] Latin American fears were eased somewhat by Cuba's pointed disavowal of any intention to intervene in the hemisphere; the Cubans argued effectively that they had come to the aid of a legitimate government—at the request of that government—to help it repel foreign aggression. In sum, the Angolan expedition had little effect on Cuba's main policy objective in Latin America— viz., to establish normal relations with the more moderate governments of the continent.

Next to the MPLA's victory, Cuba's greatest benefit from Angola was in its relations with the Soviet Union. The compatibility of Cuban and Soviet policy in Angola, and the fact that Cuban involvement was the key to that policy's success, served to further cement the good relations Cuba has enjoyed with the USSR since the early 1970s. Since 1975 Soviet economic and military assistance to Cuba has expanded, and the military stocks supplied to Cuba have been of increasing sophistication—the delivery of MiG-23s being the most publicized example.[56]

While Cuba's actions in Angola strengthened its relationship with the USSR, they also served to expand the parameters of Cuban independence vis-à-vis its principal ally. By greatly extending Cuban influence and prestige in Africa, Angola made Cuba a more valuable spokesman for socialism among the nonaligned nations. Cuba's advocacy of socialism as the only possible solution to underdevelopment is in itself politically and ideologically valuable to the USSR. Cuba has argued that nonalignment does not mean neutrality toward imperialism or neo-imperialism, and has maintained that the socialist camp led by the USSR is the Third World's natural ally.[57] In addition, Cuba has aggressively attacked Chinese influence in the nonaligned movement by denouncing China's "three worlds" theory and its condemnation of Soviet "social imperialism" and "hegemonism." Reducing Western and Chinese influence are two of the USSR's principal objectives in its policy toward the Third World, and Cuba is proving to be an indispensable ally for achieving both these goals. This gives the Soviet Union the first truly positive benefit it has derived from its relationship with Cuba, and makes any deterioration of that relationship more costly to the Soviets. This, in turn, increases Cuba's latitude for independent action and strengthens its bilateral bargaining position with the USSR.

The increased Cuban prestige resulting from its actions in Angola also advances Cuba's efforts to diversify its international economic relations, thus reducing economic dependence on the USSR. Cuba's close relationship with the PRA is a case in point. Angola, an oil-producing nation, is potentially an alternative petroleum source for Cuba, which today depends almost totally on oil imported from the Soviet Union.[58]

Finally, by providing "internationalist" aid to Angola, Cuba is fulfilling an oft-stated obligation to repay the assistance it received from the socialist camp during the early years of its own revolution. While it is extremely unlikely that Cuba and the USSR have explicitly agreed to write off any of Cuba's massive financial debt to the USSR (over $4 billion) as a reward for Cuba's Angolan intervention, Cuba's aid to Angola puts it in a much stronger bargaining position with regard to the eventual terms of repayment.[59]

From the Soviet perspective, the benefits of the MPLA victory were also substantial. The creation of the PRA was a blow to Western, Chinese, and South African influence in sub-Saharan Africa. Moreover, Cuba's assumption of the combat burden allowed the USSR to reap these benefits while maintaining a relatively low profile, thus minimizing "linkage" problems that might threaten policies with higher priority for the Soviets.

Through cooperation, Cuba and the USSR were both able to achieve policy objectives which neither could have achieved alone. Cuba could not have quickly deployed a heavily equipped force to Angola without Soviet arms shipments—and eventually, Soviet transport—while the USSR could not have undertaken a direct combat role without risking confrontation with the United States, a deterioration of detente, and charges of Soviet imperialism. The Cuban-Soviet partnership in Angola was a perfect example of a positive-sum game. Their policy objectives, though not identical, were not in conflict, and were attainable only through cooperative action. Thus their operational policies, which evolved independently, became increasingly coordinated as the Angolan civil war intensified.

Not surprisingly, Cuba paid the greatest price for the Angolan intervention in its relations with the United States. One of the principal goals of Cuban foreign policy since 1972 has been to normalize relations with the United States in order to diminish the U.S. military threat to Cuba (thus reducing its dependence on the Soviet "nuclear umbrella") and to further diversify Cuban foreign trade (thus reducing Cuba's economic dependence on the USSR). In the years immediately prior to the Angolan civil war, substantial progress had been made toward normalization, but the Cuban intervention in Angola abruptly halted that process.

During the 1960s the United States had advanced the impossible demand that Cuba sever its military relations with the USSR as a precondition for U.S.-Cuban normalization. As pressure for normalization grew in the United States, this demand was quietly jettisoned. After Angola the United States made an equally impossible demand—the complete withdrawal of Cuban troops from Africa. Since it was obviously unrealistic to expect Cuba to forfeit its highly successful African policy in exchange for relatively minor trade relations with the United States, this demand had a preemptive character, ruling out any chance of normalization. That was probably its intent. Except for direct military intervention, refusal to normalize relations was literally the only sanction the United States could impose on Cuba. Having no economic or diplomatic relations with Cuba, the United States had no leverage.

One strategy devised by the Ford administration to block further Cuban intervention in Africa was to threaten to provoke an international crisis. The occasion for unveiling this strategy came in early 1976 with a wave of rumors that Cuba intended to intervene next in Namibia. Secretary of State Kissinger warned that the United States would not tolerate a second Cuban intervention, and that the Administration was reviewing contingency plans for direct military action against Cuba. Calculated leaks from the Administration listed naval blockade, air strikes, and invasion as among the contingencies being discussed.[60]

By actively considering military action against Cuba, the United States was threatening to abrogate the 1962 U.S.-Soviet agreement that ended the Cuban missile crisis. That agreement provided for the withdrawal of Soviet missiles in exchange for a U.S. pledge not to attack Cuba. In fact, if Kissinger was seriously threatening U.S. retaliation for new Cuban intervention in Africa, it meant that the

United States had already decided it was prepared to violate the 1962 agreement. The implications of Kissinger's pronouncement for U.S.-Soviet relations were not unforeseen. A State Department official confirmed to the author at the time that the implied threat to risk a new superpower confrontation was fully intentional. No doubt the objective of this new policy was to convince the USSR of the seriousness of U.S. resolve, and thus motivate the Soviets to restrain Cuba.

Kissinger's approach was sophisticated, albeit dangerous, in that it played upon the different priorities ascribed to sub-Saharan Africa by Cuba and the Soviet Union. By threatening the USSR with an international crisis, it sought to deter further Cuban or Soviet initiatives in southern Africa (an area of low Soviet priority) by endangering detente (a high Soviet priority). In addition, by threatening Cuba militarily, Kissinger sought to inhibit any further Cuban troop commitments in Africa, since such a deployment would reduce defenses in Cuba itself. The threat of a major international crisis evaporated, however, when Cuba denied any intention of intervening in Namibia and it became clear that Cuba had begun troop withdrawals from Angola.

An assessment of the costs and benefits of Cuba's involvement in Angola would be incomplete without mention of the intervention's domestic impact in Cuba. Despite some Western predictions that Angola would prove to be "Cuba's Vietnam," popular support for the intervention remained generally high. Among strong supporters of the government, the involvement was justified by proletarian internationalism; among critics of the government, it was often supported on nationalistic grounds as an impressive display of Cuban power on a global scale. However, as the involvement in Angola has dragged on and been expanded to Ethiopia, some domestic criticisms have emerged. Without survey data, it is impossible to disentangle domestic complaints about Cuba's recent economic difficulties from complaints about its foreign involvement, but the massive exodus of Cuban refugees in early 1980 clearly demonstrates that discontent has risen sharply over the past year or two.*

There is some evidence that Angola has generated divisions within the Cuban political elite between the party and military leaderships, on the one hand, and the civilian "technocrats" in the government apparatus, on the other.[61] In several respects the

---

*At this writing the number of refugees stands at over a hundred thousand, but the exodus has not yet come to a conclusion.

intervention complicates the civilians' job of administering the Cuban economy: (1) it diverts skilled manpower from the domestic economy into the armed forces and into Cuba's foreign technical assistance program; (2) it strengthens the military's claim on a larger share of the nation's resources; and (3) it postpones the opening of U.S.-Cuban trade relations by halting the progress toward normalization of relations. There is no evidence, however, that these divisions are severe or are likely to generate any sort of crisis within the Cuban political system.

By contrast, the Cuban armed forces have benefitted considerably from Cuba's African involvement.[62] Angola provided the first real combat test for both officers and troops, as well as providing the military institution with a new "mission" to compensate for the loss of influence over domestic economic administration since 1970. Following their success in Africa, the Cuban armed forces began receiving more sophisticated Soviet weaponry (e.g., the MiG-23 fighter-interceptor). The only costs to the military have been an increase in disciplinary problems and some civilian resistance to compulsory military service, but neither of these problems has been of major proportions.

On the whole, from the Cuban perspective, the intervention in Angola was a great success. The costs were minimal and the benefits were substantial. This alone is perhaps enough to explain why the Cubans decided to repeat that intervention in Ethiopia.

IV

CUBAN INVOLVEMENT IN ETHIOPIA, 1977-1979

The context of Cuba's decision to undertake a second major troop commitment in Ethiopia differed significantly from the Angolan context. In Angola, Cuba came to the aid of a movement it had been supporting for a decade, a movement beset by external enemies of a clearly "imperialist" character—Zaire, South Africa, and the United States. In Ethiopia, Cuba came to the aid of a relatively new government with which Cuba had no historical relationship. Moreover, Cuban troops were entering into combat against troops of a nominally Marxist-Leninist Somalia which had *itself* been a recipient of Cuban military aid less than two months prior to Cuba's intervention in support of Ethiopia.

The character of Cuban-Soviet cooperation in Ethiopia was also significantly different from what it had been in Angola. Rather than evolving independent policies and eventually developing a measure of cooperation as they had in Angola, Cuba and the Soviet Union closely coordinated their military aid to Ethiopia from the outset, with the USSR playing a much more prominent role than it had in Angola. In Ethiopia the ideological lines of the conflict were much less clearly drawn and the geopolitical dimension of the conflict loomed much larger. Cuba was thus much more vulnerable to the charge of acting as a Soviet proxy.

A. THE ETHIOPIAN REVOLUTION AND GEOPOLITICS IN THE HORN OF AFRICA

The Ethiopian revolution began in February 1974 when Emperor Haile Selassie's troops refused to move against urban strikers and demonstrators. By April the military had created an alternative center of governmental power—the Coordinating Committee for the Peaceful Solution of Present Problems (later the Coordinating Committee of the Armed Forces, Police, and Ground Forces)—and in

September the emperor was deposed. The armed forces then formed a Provisional Military Administrative Government (the Dergue) headed by a Provisional Military Administrative Council (PMAC).

Having disposed of Haile Selassie, the Dergue's military commanders quickly discovered that they were by no means in agreement as to how the revolution should proceed. In November, the PMAC's moderate chairman, Aman Mikael Andom, and fifty-nine other officers were arrested and executed, purportedly for plotting a counterrevolutionary coup with U.S. assistance. The purge of Andom's group was a victory for the Dergue's left; within a month, the PMAC, now headed by Terefe Bante, announced its intention to build a socialist Ethiopia. Over the next year the Dergue nationalized most of the Ethiopian economy. The Dergue produced its first formal program in April 1976. Entitled the "Program of the National Democratic Revolution," it called for Ethiopia to "lay a strong foundation for the transition to socialism." It also included a policy position on self-determination and regional autonomy, followed in May by a nine-point policy statement aimed at a peaceful solution of the war with Eritrea.[1] The Eritrean policy proposal led to another high-level purge: in July, Major Sissy Habte, chairman of the PMAC's Foreign Affairs Committee, was executed along with a number of others for opposing the policy.

A critical turning point in the Ethiopian revolution was reached on February 3, 1977, when a PMAC meeting deteriorated into a shootout between Terefe Bante's supporters and a more radical faction led by Mengistu Haile-Mariam. Terefe was killed, his supporters were executed, and Mengistu became the PMAC's chairman.[2] The radicals' victory resulted in a sharp reorientation of Ethiopia's international position.

In addition to its own internal divisions, the Dergue faced seemingly insurmountable security problems in 1977. In the urban areas, especially Addis Ababa and Asmara, the ultra-left student-based Ethiopian People's Revolutionary Party (EPRP) was carrying out a full-scale campaign of assassination aimed at Dergue officials. In the Ogaden region the Western Somali Liberation Front (WSLF), with aid from Somalia, had taken advantage of the government's precarious position to escalate its war of secession. In Eritrea the Dergue faced armed opposition from the conservative Ethiopian Democratic Party (EDP) aided by Sudan, the Islamic Eritrean Liberation Front (ELF) aided by Sudan, Egypt, and Saudi Arabia, and the Marxist Eritrean People's Liberation Front (EPLF).

As the Ethiopian revolution moved to the left in 1976 and 1977, geopolitical alignments in the Horn of Africa were reshuffled with startling speed. Ethiopia, which had been one of the West's staunchest allies under Haile Selassie, began to move toward the USSR. The Soviet Union, which had tried with varying degrees of success to cultivate influence in Somalia and Sudan as a counterweight to U.S. influence in Selassie's Ethiopia, now sought to establish closer ties with the Dergue. Ethiopia was receptive to these overtures, both for ideological reasons and because the United States had begun slowing its arms deliveries to Ethiopia—ostensibly on human rights grounds, but more likely because of the radicalization of the revolution. Beset on all sides by enemies, the Dergue turned to the USSR for military aid in December 1976, and four months later Ethiopia severed its military relations with the United States by expelling the U.S. military mission.[3]

Somalia was particularly upset by these developments. Somalia was, after all, a self-proclaimed Marxist-Leninist state whose army was trained and equipped by the USSR. To see the Soviets suddenly begin sending military aid to a traditional Somali enemy was very disturbing, especially since Soviet arms deliveries to Somalia began to slow down—no doubt because Somalia's President Maxamed Siad Barre continued to aid the WSLF in its attempt to dismember Ethiopia at the same time the USSR was trying to improve relations with the Dergue.[4]

Somalia's disaffection from the USSR prompted renewed efforts by Sudan, Egypt (both former recipients of Soviet aid), and Saudi Arabia to wean Somalia away from the Soviet camp. They warned the Somalis of Soviet infidelity, appealed to their Islamic heritage, and enticed them with Saudi petrodollars.[5] Having been ousted from Ethiopia in April 1977, the United States joined this campaign in July by offering to supply Somalia with "defensive weapons"—an offer that was later quietly withdrawn after regular Somali troops entered the Ogaden. The geopolitical realignment in the Horn of Africa was completed in November 1977, however, when the Somalis expelled their Soviet military advisors and severed diplomatic relations with Cuba.[6]

B. CUBAN INVOLVEMENT IN THE HORN OF AFRICA

Cuban involvement in the Horn of Africa was minimal before 1976. In 1974 it had sent several dozen military technicians to Somalia, and in 1976 this contingent was reinforced by several hundred men as part of Cuba's expanded presence in Africa following the Angolan civil war.[7] As the Dergue moved to the left in 1976-1977,

Cuba came to regard the Ethiopian revolution as genuine—largely because a number of the Dergue's policies bore a striking resemblance to policies of the Cuban revolution's early years (e.g., agrarian and urban reforms, nationalizations, creation of a popular militia, and creation of the Kebele—an urban block organization reminiscent of Cuba's Committees for the Defense of the Revolution).[8]

Cuba became directly involved in the conflict between Ethiopia and Somalia in March 1977 when, during his trip to Africa, Castro acted as mediator at a summit meeting between Mengistu and Siad Barre in South Yemen. Castro proposed the creation of an anti-imperialist federation composed of South Yemen, Ethiopia, Somalia, an autonomous Ogaden, and an autonomous Eritrea. Siad Barre maintained that such a federation could be discussed only after the Ogaden was granted independence; Mengistu rejected this condition. The summit ended inconclusively, but (according to Cuban accounts) with a Somali pledge to refrain from military intervention in the Ogaden pending further negotiations.[9] Shortly thereafter Soviet President Nikolai Podgorny, also on a diplomatic tour of Africa, engaged in shuttle diplomacy between Addis Ababa and Mogadishu in an attempt to promote essentially the same solution, but also without success.

At the end of his African tour, Castro made an unscheduled visit to Moscow just after Podgorny's return. While the joint Cuban-Soviet communique following Castro's visit pledged continued Cuban and Soviet aid to southern African guerrillas,[10] the situation in the Horn was almost certainly the principal topic of the consultations. The degree of Cuban-Soviet coordination in the Horn up to this point is uncertain. On the one hand, both countries were proposing essentially the same federated solution in the Horn; on the other hand, Castro's and Podgorny's diplomatic trips through Africa did not seem to be particularly well coordinated, with Castro repeatedly upstaging the Soviet President.[11] From March 1977 onward, however, Cuban and Soviet policies were closely coordinated.

The Cuban military buildup in Ethiopia proceeded in two stages: (1) the dispatch of military advisors beginning in May 1977 after several thousand heavily armed WSLF guerrillas entered the Ogaden from Somalia, and (2) the deployment of regular combat troops in January 1978 after Somalia broke off diplomatic relations with Cuba in November 1977.

The first major escalation of the Ogaden conflict came on May 25, when three-to-six thousand WSLF guerrillas entered the Ogaden from Somalia. Somalia's decision to intensify the war was probably a response to the increased Soviet arms shipments to Ethiopia following the Dergue's ouster of the U.S. military mission in February. The Ethiopian army would require some time to switch its arms inventories from U.S. to Soviet hardware. If the Ogaden issue was to be settled militarily, the optimum time for a war (from Somalia's perspective) was during this interim—i.e., before the Ethiopians stockpiled Soviet arms and learned how to use them.

The Soviets responded to the guerrilla invasion by renewing their diplomatic drive for the federation solution and by offering Somalia increased aid if it would cease hostilities. The Saudis countered with an offer to expand their aid to Somalia twelvefold to $350 million if Siad Barre would break with Moscow. In June, as fighting in the Ogaden raged, an army of the conservative EDP entered Eritrea from Sudan under cover of artillery support from Sudanese troops massed on the border. At this point the number of Cuban military advisors in Ethiopia was only fifty.[12]

The Dergue's military position deteriorated rapidly in July. In an effort to bolster the Saudis' attempts to entice Siad Barre away from Moscow, Secretary of State Vance suggested on July 1 that the United States might be willing to provide arms to Somalia. Two weeks later, forty thousand regular Somali troops invaded the Ogaden, and in less than two weeks they had captured 112 towns and 85 percent of the region. The Soviet Union and Cuba responded by increasing their aid to Ethiopia; the Western nations, on the other hand, turned a blind eye to the invasion. Then, on July 26, the United States reiterated its interest in providing Somalia with "defensive arms" so long as they were not used in the Ogaden, and the next day Britain followed with an arms offer of its own—without the caveat about using them for defense only. The Somalis interpreted these offers as sub rosa support for their invasion, but when Somalia's intervention became too obvious to ignore, the United States withdrew its offer of arms and pressed its allies to do the same. Somalia apparently felt that U.S. hesitancy could be overcome if Somalia broke decisively with the Soviets and Cubans. On November 13 Somalia severed diplomatic relations with Cuba and expelled the Soviet military mission, which proved to be a grave miscalculation by Siad Barre. The Western nations still refused to come to his aid, and the expulsions served only to clear the way for a full Soviet-Cuban commitment to Ethiopia, which followed directly.

In January 1978 Raúl Castro traveled secretly to Addis Ababa and then to Moscow to coordinate the planned escalation of aid.[13] Over the next three months, the Cuban presence expanded from four hundred advisors to seventeen thousand regular troops (see Table 2). As noted earlier, not only were the increases in Cuban and Soviet aid to Ethiopia closely coordinated from the outset, but there was a much greater degree of cooperation than there had been in Angola. In Ethiopia, Cuban troops arrived not in converted freighters but in Soviet troop transports. Soviet military advisors numbered over a thousand, and they played a central role in planning and commanding the Ogaden campaign.[14] In Angola the role of Soviet personnel had been only marginal. Soviet-Cuban cooperation in Ethiopia was so close, in fact, that Soviet pilots were apparently assigned air defense duty in Cuba to ease the shortage of Cuban pilots, many of whom were flying combat missions in the Ogaden.[15] The Somalis, short on supplies, proved to be no match for the Cubans. Using standard Soviet assault tactics, a Cuban-Ethiopian force captured the key city of Jijiga in early March, and the Somalis fell back across the border.[16]

Table 2

CUBAN MILITARY PRESENCE IN ETHIOPIA, 1977-1980

Year/Month	Number of Troops and Military Advisors
1977	
May	50[a]
October	200
November	400
1978	
January	1000-2000
February	3000-6000
March	12,000-13,000
April	16,000-17,000[b]
1979	16,000
1980	12,000-15,000

Sources: "Western intelligence sources" as cited in *Washington Post*, May 25 and November 15, 1977; January 6, January 13, February 8, and April 1, 1978; January 21, 1979; *New York Times*, February 25, 1980.

[a]The first Cuban military personnel arrived in Ethiopia in May 1977.

[b]Estimated troop strength when the buildup stopped in late March or early April 1978.

40

The West never came to Somalia's aid, and the United States even went so far as to block the transfer of U.S. arms to Somalia from Egypt and Saudi Arabia. Western neutrality was based upon the fact that Somalia was the clear aggressor in its attempt to incorporate the Ogaden into a "Greater Somalia," and thus was violating a cardinal principle of African politics: the permanence of existing borders. Most of Africa, including the key states of Nigeria and Kenya (against whom the Somalis also had territorial claims) supported Ethiopia, despite their distaste for the Dergue. The United States repeatedly warned, however, that it would reassess its policy of neutrality if Ethiopia carried the war into Somalia. Cuba, Ethiopia, and the USSR all gave assurances that this would not happen, and it did not.[17]

The extensive nature of Cuban-Soviet coordination in the Ogaden campaign was due primarily to the strength of the Soviet commitment in Ethiopia. Unlike in Angola, the USSR transported Cuban troops, put hundreds of advisors on the ground, and joined in tactical and strategic military planning. While some might attribute this difference in Soviet behavior to the weakness of the U.S. response in Angola, it is more likely that it stemmed directly from the priorities of Soviet foreign policy. The Horn of Africa's strategic location is such that it is of "inherent importance" to the USSR. While Soviet interest in sub-Saharan Africa declined in the late 1960s, interest in the Horn remained high. Thus, while Angola was in a low priority area as far as the USSR was concerned, Ethiopia was in a high priority area—which is sufficient to account for the USSR's willingness to become involved in the Ogaden war.

Cuban motivations are less easily deciphered, but several factors probably contributed to Cuba's decision to become involved. Castro believed the Ethiopian revolution was moving in a genuinely socialist direction, and was thus attracted to the Mengistu government long before Cuba became militarily involved in the Ogaden conflict. He probably felt that, with the Dergue moving to the left, Ethiopia's and Somalia's common ideology would enable them to overcome old conflicts and enmities. His March 1977 summit meeting with Mengistu and Siad Barre was obviously intended to facilitate such a rapprochement. When Somalia resorted to force and then broke relations with Cuba, the Cuban leadership naturally held the Somalis responsible for the "fratricidal conflict" that ensued. The Cubans may also have seen Siad Barre's acceptance of Saudi petrodollars as evidence that Somalia was going the way of Egypt and China—i.e., sacrificing ideological principle for a pot of Western gold. Finally, their success in Angola may well have encouraged both Cuba and the USSR to attempt to duplicate it in Ethiopia. Given the geopolitical importance of the Horn for the USSR, the Soviets probably encouraged the Cuban involvement there, just as Cuba apparently encouraged the Soviet involvement in Angola. The Soviets could not, however, have forced a major Cuban troop commitment if the Cuban leadership had been opposed to it.

In any event, it should be noted that both Cuba and the USSR tried mightily to prevent the Ogaden war. Their military involvement was the result of their diplomatic failure. Inevitably, hostilities meant a loss of Soviet influence in one country or the other, whereas a negotiated settlement would have meant strong Soviet influence in both. Even after Somalia invaded the Ogaden in July 1977, both Cuba and the USSR continued to push for a negotiated solution while maintaining their military relations with Somalia. It was Somalia that finally terminated the Cuban and Soviet diplomatic tightrope walk in November by pushing them both solidly into the Ethiopian camp.

C. CUBA AND THE ERITREAN INSURRECTION

Once the Somalis had been expelled from the Ogaden, the Mengistu government turned its attention to the Eritrean insurgency. Mengistu's preferred strategy was to complete the consolidation of his regime by eliminating the Eritrean guerrillas militarily; to accomplish this he required the support of the Cubans and Soviets. This posed political problems for Cuba and the Soviet Union, both of whom had supported and provided material aid to the Eritreans in the late 1960s and early 1970s when they were fighting Haile Selassie. The Eritreans also had the backing of several radical Arab states with whom Cuba and the USSR sought to maintain cordial relations. Moreover, with some sixteen years of guerrilla experience and wide popular support, the Eritrean insurgents promised to be a formidable military foe.

Historically the Eritreans' greatest weakness has been internal conflicts. In 1970 the Marxist Eritrean People's Liberation Front (EPLF) split from the pro-Islamic Eritrean Liberation Front (ELF), and the rival movements spent much of the subsequent decade fighting one another. In July 1977, however, when Somalia invaded the Ogaden, the ELF and EPLF signed an agreement, at Sudanese urging, to coordinate their operations. By January 1978 the two movements controlled 90 percent of Eritrea's territory and population and held the provincial capital of Asmara under siege.

In March 1978, when the Ogaden war had just concluded, the Soviet Union appeared willing to risk the political opprobrium that would accompany its support of an Ethiopian offensive in Eritrea. The Soviets described the Eritrean insurgency in the same sort of language being used by Mengistu—e.g., the Eritreans were in league with "imperialist designs" against the Ethiopian revolution, and the insurgency was "a plot serving foreign interests."[18] The Cubans, however, were already on record as opposing a military solution to the conflict. In February, Cuban vice-president Carlos Raphael Rodríguez called for a "political solution," arguing that Eritrea was an "internal problem" of Ethiopia.[19] Given Cuba's policy of sending combat troops abroad only to protect a friendly government from external threat, the definition of Eritrea as an internal problem was tantamount to a Cuban refusal to assist Mengistu in his plans to crush the rebellion militarily. Rodríguez was even more explicit at the Belgrade conference of nonaligned foreign ministers in July:

At the present time, the problem of Eritrea is one which worries all democratic forces . . . . Cuba is not interfering in matters which are the internal affairs of Ethiopia. Regarding Eritrea, Fidel Castro has said that Cuba favors a political settlement of that issue.[20]

If the USSR had in fact been willing to give Mengistu military assistance to suppress the Eritreans, Cuba's unwillingness to collaborate ruled out such a strategy. The coordination of Cuban and Soviet policy in the Ogaden and the complementary character of Cuban and Soviet military aid to Addis Ababa constrained the policies of both nations toward Eritrea. If the Cubans were unwilling to send troops to fight the Eritreans, the Soviets could not pursue a military solution either. The result has been Soviet cooperation in Cuba's attempts to promote a negotiated settlement in Eritrea. The solution they are promoting is similar to the proposal they advanced in 1977 for the Ogaden—a federation in which Eritrea is granted regional autonomy, but in which Ethiopia's territorial integrity is preserved. While both the ELF and EPLF rejected the federation solution, they indicated a willingness to open negotiations in mid-1978, and representatives of both movements were in contact with Soviet and Cuban officials.[21]

The Mengistu government, however, was intractable. Mengistu travelled to Havana in April 1978, where he denounced the Eritreans as "secessionists," "reactionaries," and "agents of imperialism." He promised to "eliminate" them, and called upon the Cubans to help him in that endeavor. Castro reiterated the Cuban position that Eritrea was an internal matter of Ethiopia that ought to be settled peacefully,[22] but Mengistu was not persuaded. When Dergue vice-chairman Col. Atnafu Abate returned from a tour of Eritrea in late 1977 recommending a political settlement, he was executed as a CIA agent. Finally, in July 1978, while Cuba and the USSR were still trying to promote negotiations, the Ethiopian army launched a major offensive in Eritrea.

These events led to rumors that Cuba and the USSR favored a change in the Dergue's leadership. In the Spring of 1978, Cuba arranged for the secret return to Ethiopia of Negedu Gobezi, leader of the outlawed Me'isone (All-Ethiopian Socialist Movement). (The Me'isone, who had supported the Dergue before Mengistu's accession to power, were the original authors of the Dergue's 1976 nine-point policy statement proposing regional autonomy for Eritrea.) The Cubans were caught in this maneuver, however, and the Cuban ambassador was expelled from the country.[23]

In December the six-month-old Ethiopian offensive gained a major victory with the recapture of Keren--the Eritrean city which had been the headquarters of the liberation forces. This by no means ended the war, however, as both the ELF and ELPF announced a return to their earlier strategy of "protracted people's war."[24] While a purely military solution to the Eritrean conflict is no more likely now than before, the weakened military position of the Eritrean forces may make them more willing to sacrifice their demands for independence and negotiate some sort of regional autonomy. It is significant that the Ethiopian offensive during the last half of 1978 was aimed almost exclusively at areas controlled by the Islamic ELF; territory of the Marxist EPLF was largely unaffected. Assuming that the Marxist EPLF would probably be more amenable to a negotiated settlement with the Dergue, the Ethiopian offensive may have been calculated to improve the prospects for a political settlement.

Cuban and Soviet military personnel continue to refrain from any direct involvement in the Eritrean fighting,[25] though obviously their training and arming of Ethiopian forces, as well as the Cuban security role in the Ogaden, is essential for enabling the Ethiopians to conduct the Eritrean war. The likelihood of any more extensive Cuban or Soviet role in Eritrea is remote, unless there is some direct foreign intervention on the Eritreans' behalf—from Sudan, for example.

Eritrea provides an interesting context for examining not only Soviet-Cuban cooperation but also Cuba's relations with a host country. Though both Cuba and the Soviet Union obviously remain committed to the security of the Ethiopian revolutionary government, all three parties appear to have their own policy preferences with regard to Eritrea. Whatever the mutual dependencies of the three, none has surrendered its autonomy; yet precisely because of their dependencies, each is constrained to follow a policy which is less than optimal for it. The Dergue would clearly prefer to defeat the Eritreans militarily, making no political concessions whatever; but for lack of Cuban and Soviet support, it cannot. Initially at least, the Soviets seemed to prefer a military solution as well, but Cuban resistance prevented them from acting on their preference. The Cubans have consistently made clear their desire to see a negotiated settlement; while they seem to have enlisted Soviet support for this solution, the Dergue has been unyielding. Ironically, Cuban troops in the Ogaden enable the Dergue to pursue a policy in Eritrea which the Cubans oppose. Simple explanations in terms of Cuban "proxies" and Ethiopian "puppets" do not do justice to the complexity of such relationships.

During late 1978 and early 1979, the number of Cuban troops in Ethiopia declined gradually from a high of seventeen thousand to approximately thirteen thousand. This reduction merely reflects the fact that fewer troops are needed to maintain security in the Ogaden than were required to expel the Somali army. The Dergue is only slightly more secure now than it was in early 1978, and no substantial Cuban troop withdrawal is likely in the foreseeable future. Without a political settlement in Eritrea, the liberation forces will be able to conduct a long and costly guerrilla war in that region. In the Ogaden the WSLF remains active with continuing aid from Somali, and over the past six months it has stepped up its guerrilla attacks on Ethiopian forces.[26] There is also the possibility of another Somali thrust in the Ogaden. The Soviet intervention in Afghanistan has prompted the United States to reassess its decision not to provide arms to Somalia. Heretofore, such assistance was contingent upon Somalia abandoning its territorial claims on its neighbors. Now the frantic search for allies and military bases in the Persian Gulf area has led the United States to abandon this precondition.[27] If Siad Barre responds favorably to the new U.S. proposals, the effect may be to drag the United States into a second Ogaden war. But even if this worst-case scenario does not materialize, the creation of a military relationship between Somalia and the United States will certainly be perceived by Ethiopia as a new threat to its security, and the possibility of any significant Cuban withdrawal will then be postponed indefinitely.

D. THE COSTS AND BENEFITS OF INTERVENTION

On balance, intervention in Ethiopia proved to be a good deal more costly to Cuba than its intervention in Angola. While the introduction of Cuban troops prevented Somalia from seizing the Ogaden—an eventuality which would probably have caused the fall of the Mengistu government—it by no means solved the Dergue's overall security problems. The Dergue continues to be plagued with internal divisions (much more so than the MPLA), and despite its recent military successes in Eritrea, it still faces a well-entrenched, self-supporting insurgency there. In short, despite the Cuban presence the basic security of the Dergue continues to be much more tenuous than the MPLA's.

Diplomatically, Cuba paid an immediate price for its Ethiopian intervention with its expulsion from Somalia. The principal Cuban (and Soviet) objective of building good relations with Ethiopia while maintaining good relations with Somalia was lost when their attempts to promote a negotiated settlement in the Ogaden failed. The Cuban intervention has also entailed wider diplomatic costs. In Angola, despite U.S. attempts to brand the Cubans as Soviet "mercenaries," most nonaligned nations viewed the Cuban decision to intervene as both independent and principled. Thus the respect Cuba gained by demonstrating its military potency was not blemished by a belief that it was projecting its power abroad in pursuit of narrow national interests (either Soviet or Cuban). In Ethiopia, however, the diplomatic equation was more complex and the outcome for Cuba less positive. The harshness of the Dergue's internal policies (e.g., frequent executions of dissident Dergue members and the waging of a "red terror" against the EPRP) made the Ethiopian government unpopular internationally. In addition, the Soviet Union's readiness to replace the United States as Ethiopia's patron, even at the expense of its friendship with Somalia, struck many observers as crass geopolitical jockeying. Cuba's willingness to cooperate closely with the USSR to preserve the Dergue, forsaking both Somalia and the Eritreans in the process, gave credence to the argument that Cuban policy was being set in Moscow. In short, while Angola increased respect for both Cuba's power and its motives, Ethiopia added little to the former while detracting considerably from the latter. The suspicions about Soviet motives in Africa harbored by many nonaligned countries tended to be generalized to Cuba.

Little of this sentiment was publicly expressed in Africa, however. The Cuban-Soviet intervention received tacit support from the

OAU, and even from such pro-Western nations as Kenya, Zambia, and Nigeria. This was due to the ability of Cuba and the USSR to justify their intervention as a defense of established borders—a near-sacred principle in African politics. Nevertheless, the changed perception of Cuban motives surfaced in the Summer of 1978 in both the OAU and at the Belgrade meeting of foreign ministers of the nonaligned nations. In the OAU, Nigerian head of state Olusegum Obasanjo thanked Cuba for its aid to Africa, but warned the Cubans not to overstay their welcome in Africa lest they be regarded as the instruments of a new imperialism.[28] Cuba's Ethiopian intervention also occasioned heated debate at Belgrade, where President Tito charged that Cuban intervention served the interests of Soviet expansion, and Egypt sought to organize a boycott of the 6th Nonaligned Summit scheduled for Havana. Cuba prevailed in this debate (a resolution implicitly critical of Cuba's actions was rejected and the Havana site for the summit was reaffirmed), but its very occurrence demonstrated that Cuba's diplomatic position had eroded.[29]

This erosion was aggravated by Cuba's staunch support of Vietnam in the UN debate in early 1979 over Vietnam's role in the overthrow of the Pol Pot regime in Kampuchea. In this case Cuba's solidarity with its longtime friend took precedence over its support for the principle of territorial integrity, which no doubt had the effect of making Cuba's defense of the same principle in Ethiopia appear to be more expedient than sincere. It is significant that the compromise UN resolution on Kampuchea, authored by the nonaligned nations, was opposed by Cuba even though criticism of Vietnam was only implicit in the call for the withdrawal of foreign troops.[30]

Another cost to Cuba of its increased involvement in Africa during 1978 was a loss of Canadian support. In June, Canada terminated its economic assistance programs to Cuba—programs amounting to $4.4 million in technical aid and $10 million in trade credits. While not a crippling blow to the Cuban economy, the loss of Canadian aid aggravated Cuba's difficult hard currency trade position.[31]

As in the case of Angola, Cuba's intervention in Ethiopia derailed the process of normalizing U.S.-Cuban relations. When the Carter administration took office in 1977, the normalization process which had been interrupted by Angola was resumed. The Carter administration lifted the ban on U.S. tourism in Cuba, halted intelligence overflights of the island, successfully negotiated a fishing treaty with Cuba, and finally agreed to an exchange of diplomatic Interests Sections.[32] The intention to proceed with full normalization was clear on both sides, but Cuba's intervention in Ethiopia halted the process completely. When the Carter administration took office, Secretary of State Vance explicitly stated that there were no preconditions to a normalization of U.S.-Cuban relations; after Ethiopia, Kissinger's precondition of a total Cuban withdrawal from Africa was reasserted, signalling the end of the new Administration's interest in normalization.[33]

If Ethiopia made the United States suspicious of Cuban intentions in Africa, the effect it had on the U.S. perception of Soviet intentions was much greater: Ethiopia, along with other purported Soviet political gains (or U.S. losses) in South Yemen, Afghanistan (1978), Kampuchea, and Iran, catalyzed a major debate over the shape of "post-Vietnam" U.S. foreign policy. At issue was how the United States should respond to perceived "challenges," given the recognition that U.S. power to influence foreign events is not unlimited. One of the main elements in this debate was Cuban-Soviet cooperation in Africa, particularly in Ethiopia.[34]

The reverberations of the Cuban intervention are well illustrated by the curious case of the MiG-23s and the pseudo-crisis of the Soviet "combat brigade" in Cuba. In April 1978 Cuba received several MiG-23 fighter aircraft from the USSR. Since 1970 the USSR had been providing equipment to upgrade the level of Cuban military technology; the replacement of Cuban MiG-21s with the more sophisticated MiG-23 was consistent with this policy. In some configurations, however, the MiG-23 is capable of delivering nuclear weapons. Despite the fact that there was no evidence that the Cuban MiG-23s were "nuclear-capable" or that there were any nuclear weapons in Cuba, some U.S. commentators interpreted the delivery of the MiG-23s as equivalent to the 1962 missile crisis. The Administration resisted calls to reenact the 1962 confrontation, but it did resume SR-71 reconnaissance overflights of Cuba in an effort to silence its critics.[35]

It is unlikely that there would have been a MiG-23 controversy if Cuba had not had troops in Africa. Yet neither Cuba nor the MiG-23s were the real target of the polemics; they were merely the occasion for them. The real quarry of those who were most vociferous about the MiG-23s was the SALT II agreement. In the minds of many, localized politico-military conflicts between the United States and the USSR (or their friends) are inseparable from strategic arms issues. As Senate Minority Leader Howard Baker put it: "I would not support [SALT II] if I'm convinced that, treaty terms aside, the Soviet Union is laying down a challenge to the U.S. throughout the world." (He then mentioned Cuban and Soviet actions in Africa as evidence of such a challenge.)[36]

The MiG-23 "crisis," however, was minor compared to the September 1979 tempest over the Soviet "combat brigade"—a furor which came much closer to reenacting the 1962 missile crisis. Whereas the Carter administration downplayed the MiG-23 issue, its response to the "combat brigade" was to exaggerate the issue's importance— both domestically and internationally.

The origin of the controversy was a debate within the U.S. intelligence community during the Summer of 1979 over whether there had been a change in the Soviet military presence in Cuba. Senior analysts were unconvinced there had been a change, but those who found the evidence more compelling enlisted the support of Senator Richard Stone (D-Florida), who demanded and received from the Administration a pledge of further investigation. Satellite photos taken in August revealed two-to-three thousand Soviet military personnel on maneuvers near Havana.[37] The Administration took this as "unambiguous" evidence that the USSR had placed a "combat brigade" in Cuba, and began wrestling with how to handle such a politically sensitive issue. If the MiG-23s were any indication, a public revelation would produce heated rhetoric in the election-year political climate, endangering not only SALT II, but also complicating the prospects for a diplomatic resolution of the issue with the Soviets. As the Administration weighed its alternatives, Secretary Vance informed Senate Foreign Relations Committee chairman Frank Church (D-Idaho) of the new intelligence reports.[38]

Facing a stiff reelection challenge from the right because of his liberal record, Church could not resist the opportunity to strike a hardline posture. On August 30 in Boise, Church revealed the existence of the "brigade" and called upon Carter to demand its immediate removal. There was "no likelihood," he added, that SALT II would pass until the Soviet troops were withdrawn. Naturally, SALT II opponents pounced on the issue, with various presidential contenders in the rhetorical forefront of the debate. Scrambling to recover its balance, the Administration tried to sound decisive while still leaving its options open; it announced that the status quo was "unacceptable," but without specifying what measures might be taken to alter it.[39]

As the firestorm of public debate grew, existence of the "combat brigade" (i.e., a unit of regular combat troops over and above the Soviet military advisory mission which had been in Cuba since 1962) was taken for granted. Within the intelligence community, however, there was less certainty.[40] Grave doubts still existed as to the exact character of the Soviet personnel detected in August. No one could say when they arrived in Cuba, or how they could have gotten there undetected. Moreover, no one could offer a plausible theory as to their mission, or why they operated in brigade formation (a unit structure characteristic of the Cuban armed forces, but extremely unusual in the Soviet army). Such uncertainties seemed marginal in the rush of public debate. The Administration itself paid them little heed in its desire to use the troop issue to embarrass Cuba during the 6th Summit of the Nonaligned Nations which, fortuitously, was convening in Havana just as the "troops" were discovered.

Despite demands for decisive action from hardliners seeking to resurrect the heroic days of the 1962 missile crisis, the "crisis" dragged on for over a month while U.S. and Soviet officials conferred. The general expectation was that the Soviets would offer some concession, even if merely cosmetic, in order to assure the survival of SALT II, but they did not. Both Cuba and the USSR insisted that there was no "combat brigade"—i.e., that U.S. satellites had photographed activities of the Soviet advisory mission which had been in Cuba—unchanged in size or function—since 1962. The Soviets explained that they were not about to make concessions to resolve a wholly artificial crisis.[41]

Such categorical denials prompted a reexamination of the caveats in the intelligence estimates—caveats which had previously been swept aside in the public drama of crisis.[42] The intelligence community could not rule out the possibility that the Cuban and Soviet claims were true. Moreover, such an explanation would account for how the "brigade" could have slipped into Cuba undetected, why the Soviet troops were operating as a brigade in the first place, and what purpose they could possibly serve. Those loose ends, which had seemed so minor at first, suddenly loomed large. Their implication was that the major premise of the crisis—that the Soviets had changed the status quo with a military initiative in Cuba—might be mistaken. The Soviets were unwilling to do more than reiterate that the Soviet personnel in Cuba were an advisory mission and would remain so. Thus the "unacceptable" status quo, whatever it was, became "acceptable" because the Carter administration could not alter it. Its acceptance was rather transparently camouflaged with an increased U.S. military presence in the Caribbean and a made-for-television landing of eighteen hundred marines at Guantanamo naval base. During the landing, the Cuban armed forces around Guantanamo were not even put on alert.[43]

CUBAN INVOLVEMENT IN ETHIOPIA, 1977-1979

The pseudo-crisis of the Soviet "combat brigade" was essentially a replay of the MiG-23 and Shaba II* crises before it, and like those earlier crises it was largely a by-product of Soviet and Cuban policy in Africa. As in the Shaba II crisis, the Administration jumped to the worst possible conclusion on the basis of equivocal intelligence, based its conduct of the crisis on this worst-case conclusion, and in the end was forced to implicitly acknowledge that it may have been mistaken about the facts. This tendency to assume the worst was probably an inevitable result of the deterioration in U.S.-Cuban relations after Cuba's Ethiopian intervention. Frustrated by Cuba's success and unable to devise a policy to counter it, the Carter administration developed an acute sensitivity to any issue involving the Cubans. In the brigade crisis, the cost of casting Cuba as the *bete noire* of U.S. foreign policy was high. Not only did the Administration look foolish, but U.S.-Soviet relations were also severely damaged. From the Soviet perspective, the creation of the crisis suggested that the Carter administration was an irresponsible and unreliable partner in detente. By devaluing detente, the crisis contributed to a set of global circumstances wherein the Soviets were willing to risk losing detente altogether in the pursuit of other interests in Afghanistan.

*See pp. 26-27 above.

V

THE PROSPECTS FOR CUBAN INVOLVEMENT IN AFRICA

Cuba's involvement in Africa has given it a degree of global influence that is rare among small states. Since it has been able to attain this influence at relatively low cost, Cuba is not likely to abandon its new role as a world actor. However, the balance sheet on its intervention in Ethiopia suggests that if Cuba participates in further military expeditions of this type it may reach a point of diminishing returns. Cuban-Soviet relations are so close today that additional cooperative ventures can hardly strengthen that relationship. But new interventions undertaken in concert with the USSR (as they would almost have to be) would almost certainly reinforce Third World suspicions about the motivations and independence of Cuban policy, and much of the influence Cuba has gained since 1972 among the nonaligned nations could be lost.

With between one-fifth and one-quarter of its regular armed forces already deployed in Africa (about half the troops there are reservists),[1] the size of Cuba's military becomes a limit on its ability to make additional troop commitments without withdrawing some troops from Angola or Ethiopia.

Cuba's need to maintain large troop contingents in Angola and Ethiopia to assure the security of those governments may have corrosive effects on the domestic political situation in Cuba. There is no end in sight for either of these commitments, and Cuban forces continue to sustain casualties in both countries. Further troop deployments might prove difficult for the Cuban leadership to justify on the home front at a time when domestic economic difficulties are generating more popular discontent than at any time since 1970.*

All these considerations suggest that rampant Cuban intervention is highly unlikely. Any future interventions are likely to be carefully calculated to minimize the sorts of costs that accrued to Cuba

*As noted earlier, the severity of Cuba's internal problems was graphically illustrated in early 1980 when over a hundred thousand Cuban refugees came to the United States via the sealift from Mariel harbor.

in Ethiopia—i.e., they will occur only where there are prospects of advancing Cuba's overall objectives at comparatively low cost.

A. CUBAN POLICY IN SOUTHERN AFRICA

The most likely arena for increased Cuban military involvement is southern Africa, primarily because that is the region in which there is most likely to be increased military conflict in the future. It is also an area in which Cuba's involvement has been legitimated —in Namibia, by the nearly universal condemnation of apartheid and South African rule there, and in Zimbabwe, by the failure of Abel Muzorewa's internal settlement regime to achieve any measure of international acceptance, which served to justify Cuba's aid to the Patriotic Front before the Lancaster House agreements.

Cuba has long supported the liberation struggles in both Namibia and Zimbabwe, but it has provided arms and military advisors to SWAPO and the Patriotic Front only since 1976. Before the Angolan war, SWAPO cooperated with UNITA forces along Angola's Namibian border. This was largely a tactical necessity (neither the MPLA or FNLA had guerrillas operating in that area), but Cuba's hostility to UNITA ruled out any substantial assistance to SWAPO. In Zimbabwe, the perennial conflict between Joshua Nkomo's ZAPU and Robert Mugabe's ZANU (the two movements which comprised the Patriotic Front) seems to have been the principal reason for Cuba's non-involvement.

The general expansion of Cuba's presence in Africa following the Angolan war included the beginning of assistance programs to both SWAPO and the Patriotic Front. Cuban military advisors established guerrilla training camps for SWAPO in Angola and for the Front in Tanzania and Mozambique.[2] Cuban policy, however, consistently ruled out the use of regular combat troops in either Namibia or Zimbabwe. In 1976, Cuban vice-president Rodriguez said that Cuban troops would not intervene in Namibia, and he reasserted this position in early 1977, when he told a BBC interviewer that Cuban troops would not become directly involved in wars of national liberation.[3] Castro himself confirmed this policy during his March 1977 Africa trip: "It is not Cuba's intention to send soldiers to fight in any part of southern Africa. Independence is never delivered from abroad. The people concerned must fight for their independence."[4]

At the same time, however, Castro left open the question of Cuba's future role by declaring that Cuban policy in southern Africa would be largely determined by the "Front Line" states (Tanzania,

Angola, Mozambique, Zambia, and Botswana).[5] In the summer of 1977, when Rhodesia stepped up its air and ground attacks on Zambia and Mozambique, Cuba offered military aid to Zambia to help protect its borders. President Kaunda declined to accept, but he threatened on several occasions to turn to Cuba for assistance if the West could not restrain Rhodesia.[6] In Namibia, Cuba helped convince SWAPO to accept the UN plan for independence, but if that formula fails, SWAPO leader Sam Nujoma has said that SWAPO reserves the right to ask for direct Cuban aid.[7]

In Zimbabwe, the successful conclusion and implementation of the historic Lancaster House agreements has dramatically reduced the immediate prospects for war in southern Africa. Against all odds, British Foreign Secretary Lord Carrington managed to conjure an agreement for elections and peaceful transfer of power which Commissioner Lord Soames was able to carry out, and which South Africa was obliged to tolerate.[8] Though it may have been a peculiar balance of forces between the combatants that made these agreements possible, they nevertheless demonstrate the sophistication of British diplomacy in the region—especially in contrast to that of the United States. Before the Lancaster House negotiations began, the United States was poised to abandon the UN economic sanctions imposed on Rhodesia, giving the Muzorewa regime de facto recognition.[9] The recent elections appear to indicate the Muzorewa's legitimacy was very attenuated indeed. The United States was saved from another diplomatic debacle in Africa only by the timeliness of the British initiatives.

The contrast between the U.S. and British policies is instructive. While Britain was guided primarily by a desire to find a regionally viable solution, the United States was responding almost exclusively to the East-West dimension of the conflict. Despite its conservatism the Thatcher government recognized that Muzorewa could not survive the combined hostility of the Patriotic Front and the Front Line states.[10] Moreover, the British recognized that their *own* interests would be more damaged by trying to prop Muzorewa up than by the electoral victory of the Patriotic Front.

With regard to Cuban and Soviet involvement, it is noteworthy that neither sought to block or subvert the Lancaster House accords. Because both were sensitive to their need to maintain legitimacy for their involvement in the region, they took their cues from the Front Line states, whose participation in hammering out the accords was at least as critical as Britain's.[11]

Mugabe's overwhelming electoral victory realized the worst fears of South Africa and of Zimbabwe's conservative whites. The electoral division of the Patriotic Front did not lead to its defeat (as many had anticipated), but instead gave control of the government to the Front's more radical faction. Yet this was hardly a victory for the Soviet Union (or conversely, a defeat for the West). Most aid from the socialist camp to the Zimbabwe liberation movement has been channelled to Nkomo because of Mugabe's past flirtations with Peking.[12] Mugabe's independence from the Soviet Union, combined with his deliberately moderate and conciliatory approach to governing, may make his election the best outcome the West could have realistically hoped for. So long as South Africa abides by its pledge to refrain from military intervention in Zimbabwe, the prospects for peace seem reasonably good.

There are, however, less optimistic scenarios. The focus of the struggle for national liberation in Africa will now shift to South Africa itself. As the newest member of the Front Line states, Zimbabwe will eventually take an active part in that struggle. Thus there is still a real potential for armed conflict between Zimbabwe and South Africa—just as there is between Angola and South Africa. Should such conflict erupt, the probability of a major Cuban response is greater now that the legitimacy of the Mugabe government has been internationally certified. Whereas Cuban policy ruled out direct intervention against the Muzorewa regime, that policy would certainly sanction a direct effort in defense of Mugabe if he were to request it.

A complicating factor in all this is whether the USSR, which has always been more wary of Mugabe than the Cubans have, would support a major deployment of Cuban troops in Mugabe's defense. On the basis of the Angolan precedent, it appears they would, but the Cubans might well have to convince them that it was desirable.

A more immediate threat to peace in southern Africa is in Namibia. While it is possible that a solution modeled on the Lancaster accords may be reached there, it is not very likely. If final agreement is not reached on the UN plan for peaceful transition to majority rule in Namibia, SWAPO will undoubtedly escalate the guerrilla war with logistical support from Cuba and Angola. South Africa may then be tempted to carry the war into SWAPO base areas in southern Angola, bringing the South Africans into direct confrontation with Cuban troops. Cuba might then no longer feel any compunction about respecting international frontiers. Given the nearly universal condemnation of South African rule in Namibia, direct intervention by Cuba would probably generate little international criticism if it was provoked by a major South African attack on Angola. One can only

CUBA'S POLICY IN AFRICA, 1959-1980

hope that the South Africans, chastened by events in Zimbabwe, will avoid such provocations.

Under any circumstances, however, Cuban policy toward both Zimbabwe and Namibia will depend largely upon the climate of international opinion in the UN, the OAU, and especially among the Front Line states. The Cubans will not commit regular combat troops into any conflict without substantial regional support and a plausible claim for the legitimacy of their effort. Though the Cuban and Soviet roles in southern Africa have thus far been primarily military, neither country has been hostile to negotiated settlements which include the guerrilla movements. The Cubans have already cooperated once with Western diplomatic efforts by helping to convince SWAPO to accept the UN plan for Namibia, and neither Cuba nor the USSR sought to subvert the Lancaster House negotiations. Indeed the Cubans even gave a cautious endorsement to the final agreement.[13]

The extent of Cuba's future military involvement in southern Africa will thus depend (as it did in Angola and Ethiopia) upon whether or not internal conflicts become internationalized. Neither the Cubans nor the Soviets will allow the nationalist movements in Zimbabwe or Namibia to be defeated militarily by an influx of foreign arms or foreign troops.

B. SOUTH YEMEN AND THE CONFLICTS OF THE ARABIAN PENINSULA

The third largest Cuban military mission abroad is in the Democratic People's Republic of Yemen (DPRY-South Yemen). The first Cuban military advisors, about 200 strong, arrived in the DPRY in 1973 to train both the Yemeni army and the Dhofari guerrillas fighting in Oman. Later that year, when Iran sent 1,200 counterinsurgency troops into Oman in a concerted effort to crush the guerrillas, the Cuban presence in South Yemen was tripled to approximately 600-700 men. The threat of an Iranian and/or Saudi attack on Yemen caused Yemeni support for the Dhofaris to wane over the next few years, and as the rebellion collapsed and the threat of war receded, the Cuban advisory mission dwindled to its original size of about 200.[14]

The most persistent foreign policy issue for South Yemen has been its relations with North Yemen. Both Yemeni regimes regard Yemen as a single country, and both seek to unify that country under their own leadership. But while the South is the most radical Arab country in the world, the North is ruled by conservatives closely allied with and dependent upon Saudi Arabia. Not surprisingly, conflict between the two Yemens has been endemic since South Yemen gained independence in 1967. The North Yemenis, with Saudi assistance, have trained and armed exile armies that periodically launch assaults on the PDRY, while the South Yemenis supply arms to leftist guerrillas operating in North Yemen. This mutual antagonism erupted in a border war in 1972, which was ended by Arab League mediation. In an effort to avoid future warfare, the two Yemens signed a unification agreement, but their disparate ideologies have prevented them from achieving more than an uneasy armistice.[15]

In 1978 the relations between north and south became the focus of political conflict within the PDRY. On June 24, President al-Ghashmi of North Yemen was killed by a bomb contained in the briefcase of an emissary from PDRY leader Salem Robea Ali. Though the assassination did not provoke war between the two Yemens, it did precipitate armed conflict in South Yemen between forces loyal to Robea Ali and those of his opponents in the PDRY leadership. Robea Ali was deposed and replaced by Prime Minister Ali Nasser Mohammed.[16] The change in leadership was generally perceived as a victory for the "pro-Soviet" faction in South Yemen, and indeed the PDRY's relations with the USSR did improve. In the wake of this crisis, the Cuban military mission was expanded to about 300-400 advisors.[17]

In February 1979 a new border war erupted between North and South Yemen. Each side accused the other of aggression, but because the fighting occurred in a remote mountainous region, no one could say for sure who was responsible for the war.[18] The United States had rarely paid much attention to either Yemen, but after the June 1978 crisis it began coordinating its policy in the area with Saudi Arabia; the North Yemeni armed forces were equipped with several hundred million dollars worth of U.S. armaments paid for by the Saudis.[19] The 1979 border war was perceived by the Carter administration as a major global crisis. Among U.S. policymakers, the combination of the Cuban and Soviet involvement in Ethiopia and the downfall of the Shah in Iran evoked visions of an "arc of crisis" running through the heart of the oil-producing Middle East. Yemen was situated in the middle of that "arc."

U.S. policymakers perceived the war as one more stage in an orchestrated Soviet campaign to expand its influence at Western expense—the lineal descendent of Soviet successes in Angola and Ethiopia. They feared the emergence of a united Marxist-Leninist Yemen allied with the Soviets, threatening Saudi security and controlling the Bab al-Mandab Strait (the fifteen-mile-wide channel linking the Red Sea with the Gulf of Aden). Deeply shaken by the sudden collapse of the Shah's regime in Iran, the Saudis were no less nervous.[20]

Shortly after the war began, the Saudis indicated to Washington their intention to intervene in the war on the side of North Yemen, and asked for permission to use their stock of U.S. weapons in the conflict. The United States agreed, promised to replace any arms the Saudis provided to Yemen, and stepped up its own arms shipments to Yemen (sending $400 million worth in two weeks). Since the Yemenis were not trained to utilize the equipment being deployed, U.S., Egyptian, and Jordanian military advisors were sent to Sana to train them. To reassure the Saudis of American resolve, the Administration dispatched the aircraft carrier Constellation to the Persian Gulf.[21]

While the United States and its regional allies were feverishly expanding their military involvement in the region, the Carter administration advised the Soviet Union not to increase logistical support for Aden, lest it undermine the Arab League's attempts to mediate the conflict.[22] Not surprisingly, the Soviets and Cubans were unimpressed by the logic of the U.S. position. Both stepped up their aid to the PDRY, and within a few weeks the Cuban military advisory mission had doubled to nearly 700 men.[23] No regular Cuban troops were deployed, however, and the Cuban and Soviet advisors were careful not to become directly involved in the fighting, which was taking place on the northern side of the border.[24]

Thus the stage was set for a reenactment of the Angolan and Ethiopian wars. Had North Yemen or Saudi Arabia carried the war into South Yemen, there is little doubt the Cubans and Soviets would have responded with military support for the PDRY. Such an escalation was avoided because North Yemen was unwilling to serve as the staging ground for a superpower confrontation.[25] The Arab League's mediation efforts succeeded in late March (as they had before in 1972), bringing the war to an end, and a week later North and South Yemen signed another agreement to move toward unification. The Carter administration was somewhat taken aback by this sudden turn of events, but pledged that the promised military aid would be dispatched to Sana nonetheless.[26] To date the Cuban military presence in Aden has remained at its augmented level.

In Angola and Ethiopia, U.S. policymaking was distorted by the Cuban and Soviet involvements; in Yemen, U.S. policymakers were virtually blinded. Because both Cuban and Soviet advisors were present in South Yemen, the Carter administration automatically assumed that the 1979 war was a new global challenge, rather than simply a repetition of the 1972 war. The intricacies of the region's political dynamics received scant attention as the United States rushed to reassure Saudi Arabia by enlisting wholeheartedly behind North Yemen. Thus, even though the government in Sana was one of the most unpopular and unstable regimes in the region, the Carter administration chose to wager its prestige on Sana's survival at a time when U.S. intelligence estimates were predicting that the government could not survive its *internal* opposition for more than six months.[27] Yet survive it did, and in late 1979 it turned to the Soviet Union for military assistance—much to the chagrin of the United States.[28]

There is no mystery in this, if one looks beyond the cold war stereotypes that guided U.S. policy in the area. Though North and South Yemen are poles apart ideologically, and the North is virtually a client of Saudi Arabia, Sana's ethnic and cultural ties are with its Marxist brother to the south—not its Saudi cousin to the north. Indeed Saudi hegemony in North Yemen is a source of continual tension and resentment.[29] The attempts to unify North and South Yemen, however abortive, reflect the fact that ethnic and cultural conflicts in the region are at least as potent as ideological ones. The vision of a united Yemen capable of exerting its autonomy from Saudi economic and political influence does not appeal only to the Marxists in the south.

There is potential for a sharp expansion of the Cuban and Soviet military presence in South Yemen if war between the Yemens should resume. Cuba and the USSR can be expected to provide whatever military assistance the PDRY requires to protect its borders—up to and including regular Cuban combat forces. It is unlikely, however, that either Cuba or the Soviet Union will encourage South Yemen to renew hostilities. A more promising strategy, which the USSR seems to be pursuing, is to woo the North with the prospect of a united or federated Yemen powerful enough to break Saudi Arabia's hegemony in the area. North Yemen is not prepared to break its lucrative ties with the West, but neither is it willing to act as a Western bulwark in the "arc of crisis."

C. GUERRILLA WAR IN THE WESTERN SAHARA

When Spain abandoned its western Sahara colony in 1975, both Morocco and Mauritania laid claim to the region and dispatched troops to occupy it. There was much speculation about whether the two nations might go to war over the territory, but scant attention was paid to the Polisario guerrillas—a small group of Saharan nationalists who vowed to wage war against both occupiers. With aid from Algeria and the support of most of the Sahara's populace, the Polisario proved adept at both desert warfare and international diplomacy. In July 1979 the OAU adopted a resolution calling for self-determination in the region. The Polisario promptly formed a provisional government (the Saharan Arab Democratic Republic), and by October had gained recognition from thirty-four governments. Faced with the OAU's July resolution and the mounting cost of the war, Mauritania renounced its claim to the western Sahara in August and withdrew. Morocco then occupied the entire territory.[30]

The war with the Polisario has become an albatross for Morocco's King Hassan. Despite an estimated expenditure of $1.5 million a day, Morocco is losing. Saudi Arabia has borne part of the war's financial burden, but Morocco is nevertheless deeply in debt, and the Polisario are inflicting casualties on the Moroccans at a rate of several hundred per week. In large-scale battles, which are becoming more frequent, it has not been uncommon for Morocco to lose 300-400 killed in a few days. U.S. intelligence analysts regard the military situation as dismal, and its deterioration imperils Hassan's domestic political position.[31] The most serious danger, however, is that the war might expand into a general conflict between Morocco and Algeria as Moroccan troops engage in "hot pursuit" of Polisario guerrillas operating from bases in southern Algeria.

Until late 1979 the official U.S. position on the western Sahara was one of neutrality. The western Sahara was hardly an area of strategic importance, and Washington sought to avoid choosing sides between Morocco and Algeria.[32] Hassan, however, is a particularly important U.S. ally: he not only endorsed the Camp David accords, but he also sent troops to Zaire during both Shaba incursions. Thus when Hassan asked the United States for military aid in October 1979, the Carter administration felt obliged to comply, even though Hassan was explicit about his intent to use the arms in the Sahara war. The administration's embarrassingly transparent justification for supplying the arms was that they would enable Hassan to enter into negotiations with the Polisario by strengthening Morocco's military position,[33] even though Hassan has never indicated any willingness to negotiate an end to the war. The real basis for the U.S. decision was that "global considerations" required that the United States come to the aid of its ally, however ill-advised and regionally illegitimate the Sahara war might be.

U.S. military aid will allow Morocco to prolong a war it cannot win, making the eventual denouement all the more painful and perilous for Hassan's domestic political position. Diplomatically, it ensures that the Saharan Arab Democratic Republic will be no friend of the United States, and it undermines U.S. prestige all across the continent, since it flies in the face of the OAU resolution and the policies of most African nations. A larger peril in this policy, however, is that it threatens to embroil the United States in a wider war in which it is once again aligned with the side that cannot win. If war breaks out between Morocco and Algeria, Algeria's military superiority is such that it would almost certainly win; moreover, it would have the support of most of the Third World. The temptation for the United States to come to Hassan's aid once again would be great, since the Algerians would enjoy both Cuban and Soviet support, as they have for nearly two decades. Yet any escalation of U.S. aid would surely bring a counter-escalation by Algeria's allies. The first commitment of regular Cuban combat troops abroad, it will be recalled, was to support Algeria in its 1963 border war with Morocco.

D. CONCLUSION

In southern Africa, North Africa, and the Middle East, the prospects for further Cuban military involvement depend upon the same factors that guided Cuban involvement in Angola and Ethiopia. If regional conflicts become internationalized, and the involvement of Western or pro-Western nations threatens the territorial integrity of a Cuban ally, Cuba will respond within the limits of its military capability—i.e., subject to the USSR's willingness to provide logistical support. South African intervention in Zimbabwe or a concerted South African assault on Angola could bring Cuban troops into Zimbabwe or Namibia. A new war between North and South Yemen with strong Saudi participation could bring Cuban troops into Yemen. An expansion of the war in the western Sahara into a general war between Morocco and Algeria could bring Cuban troops into Algeria. In each of these scenarios, Cuban involvement would enjoy widespread legitimacy in the Third World—legitimacy which is a necessary condition of any major Cuban troop commitment.

CUBAN FOREIGN POLICY IN A GLOBAL CONTEXT

Cuba's military involvement in Africa was the most dramatic aspect of its foreign policy during the 1970s, but it was only one dimension of that policy. The growth of Cuban influence in the Third World has been a primary objective of Cuba's foreign policy since 1972, and if Cuba has become a "small state with a big foreign policy," the deployment of combat troops abroad has been only one source of its global influence. Cuba has won its place as chairman of the Movement of Nonaligned Nations not only through military prowess, but also with a substantial foreign economic assistance program and a consistent record of advocacy on behalf of the economic concerns of Third World countries.

A. CUBA IN THE MOVEMENT OF NONALIGNED NATIONS

Though Cuba was a founding member of the Nonaligned Movement in 1961, the Cubans were only marginally involved in the movement during the 1960s. The radicalism of Cuban foreign policy during those years did not blend well with the nonaligned nations' emphasis on peaceful coexistence, and Cuban delegates to nonaligned summits tried in vain to shift the movement's focus to the issues of colonialism and global economics.[1]

As the cold war gave way to detente in the early 1970s, the urgency of the peace issue receded, but the economic position of the Third World countries continued to deteriorate. Decrying the fact that peaceful coexistence had not significantly improved their position in the global economy, the nations of the Third World banded together to demand a New International Economic Order. This more radical thrust in the Nonaligned Movement coincided with the new pragmatism of Cuba's post-1972 foreign policy. With its long record of support for a greater economic focus for the movement, Cuba naturally emerged as a leader within the Third World. Its military assistance to the MPLA solidified that leadership position. After congratulating Cuba for its actions in Angola, the 5th Summit of the

Nonaligned Nations (Sri Lanka, 1976) selected Havana as the site for the 1979 summit, following which Cuba would chair the movement until 1982.[2] U.S. attempts to portray Cuba as a Soviet puppet unworthy of nonaligned status have been unsuccessful. The criteria for nonalignment have always been notoriously loose, and Cuba's credentials as a nonaligned nation have never been seriously challenged from within the movement itself. On the contrary, Cuba's dual position as a member of both the Third World and the socialist camp is a primary source of its influence in both spheres. As a spokesman for socialism among the nonaligned, Cuba's value to the Soviet Union is much greater than it was in the 1960s, and it is equally valuable to the Nonaligned Movement as a spokesman for the Third World within the socialist camp. Despite U.S. protestations, neither the nonaligned nor the socialist countries perceive this symbiosis as inherently contradictory.

Yet the potential for tension in Cuba's broker role is great. Its economic dependence on the USSR and its reliance upon the Soviets to provide logistical support for its major military involvements inevitably link Cuban prestige with Third World perceptions of the Soviet Union. As long as the Third World perceives the Soviets as benign, Cuba's dual role is tenable. But when the perceived interests of the Soviets and the nonaligned nations are in conflict, the Cubans are caught in the middle. This has happened twice—over the issues of Kampuchea and Afghanistan. On both occasions Cuba sided with the socialist camp rather than with the Third World, with noticeable damage to its prestige among the latter.

When the nonaligned nations offered a compromise UN resolution condemning the Vietnamese intervention in Kampuchea, Cuba opposed it. The issue arose again among the nonaligned nations as they prepared for the 1979 Havana summit. The Cubans argued that Kampuchea's seat in the movement should be given to the Vietnamese-supported Heng Samrin government; the moderates, led by Yugoslavia, supported the Pol Pot regime on the grounds that the movement should not recognize a government installed by foreign intervention. The Cuban position was in the minority when the summit convened, so Cuba advanced a compromise proposal to leave the seat temporarily vacant. The moderates rejected the compromise, and the issue became the focus of the most rancorous debate of the summit. The Cuban position ultimately prevailed, but a number of delegates left Havana complaining that Cuba had manipulated the proceedings to obtain the result it desired.[3] Evidence that the Havana compromise was not a genuine consensus was quick in coming. Less than a month later, when the UN took up the issue of Kampuchea's credentials, a similar compromise proposal was soundly defeated, with a sizable bloc of nonaligned nations voting in favor of the Pol Pot delegation.[4]

The damage done to Cuban prestige by this controversy was reflected in a subsequent General Assembly election for the "Latin American seat" on the Security Council which pitted Cuba against Colombia. As chairman of the Nonaligned Movement, Cuba should have won the necessary two-thirds majority easily (Colombia was not even a member of the movement), but the election remained deadlocked through eighty-six ballots. Though it was a secret ballot election, the voting totals indicated that nearly two dozen nonaligned nations were casting ballots for Colombia.[5]

The election deadlock was eventually broken by the political repercussions of the Soviet intervention in Afghanistan. The extent to which Cuban prestige in the Third World is partially tied to Soviet prestige was quickly reflected in the balloting. In the wake of the intervention, Cuba's plurality of eighty-to-ninety votes eroded almost immediately to seventy. Faced with the prospect that it might ultimately lose the election, and prompted by a compromise initiated from within the Nonaligned Movement by India and Nigeria, Cuba withdrew from the election in favor of Mexico. Mexico won the seat on the next ballot.[6]

In 1979 a UN General Assembly resolution condemning the Soviet intervention in Afghanistan confronted Cuba with the most difficult political choice it had faced since the 1968 Soviet intervention in Czechoslovakia. Indeed the issues at stake were virtually identical. The Cubans were forced to choose between two sets of deeply held principles which had suddenly come into conflict: on the one hand, the sovereignty and territorial integrity of small states; on the other, the security and political integrity of the socialist camp—i.e., the irreversibility of socialist revolutions. Both sets of principles have been crucial for the Cubans' own security, and— not coincidentally—each is the central tenet of one of the two major groups of states with which Cuba feels affinity: the Third World and the socialist camp.

In 1968 Cuba sided with the socialist camp, though Castro's endorsement of the Soviet intervention in Czechoslovakia was highly qualified. By 1979, however, Cuba had successfully established itself as a Third World leader, and hence had much more to lose by an open endorsement of the Soviet action. For several weeks the Cubans offered no official statement whatsoever on the events in Afghanistan.

(During this period Cuban diplomats in the United States confided that they had received no instructions.)[7] When the resolution condemning the Soviet intervention in Afghanistan finally came up for debate in the UN General Assembly, Cuban ambassador Raúl Roa rose to speak against it. At no point in his brief statement, however, did Roa endorse or defend the Soviet action. On the contrary, he noted that many of Cuba's friends in the Third World were deeply disturbed by the intervention and that it posed "an historic dilemma."[8] Roa's speech concentrated primarily upon denouncing the United States, and he declared that Cuba would never join with imperialism against the Soviet Union. But the speech did little to dispel the ambiguity of Cuba's position on the intervention.

In what may be an attempt to repair its damaged prestige among the nonaligned countries, Cuba offered in March 1980 to act as a mediator between Afghanistan and Pakistan. If the offer is accepted, it would mark a major diplomatic victory for the Cubans and a successful assertion of their role as broker between the socialist camp and the Third World.

B. CUBAN AND SOVIET POLICY COORDINATION IN AFRICA

In the late 1960s, Cuban and Soviet policies toward Africa stood in marked contrast to one another. Cuba was pursuing a militant though limited policy based upon its ideological attraction to progressive regimes (e.g., Algeria, Ghana, Guinea) and national liberation movements (e.g., MPLA, PAIGC, FRELIMO); the USSR was reorienting its policy away from ideological considerations toward more geopolitical ones. As a result, Cuba was openly critical of Soviet behavior.

In the 1970s, as the direct threat to Cuba's security offered by the United States receded, Cuba began to place increasing emphasis on expanding its influence in the Third World. An expansion of Cuban military aid to Africa was one manifestation of that policy, and when Cuba's longtime friend in Angola—the MPLA—was faced with major external threats, Cuba came to its aid with military advisors and later with regular combat troops. This policy was compatible with a Soviet decision made at about the same time to provide the MPLA with heavy weapons, and after the summer of 1975, Cuban and Soviet aid to Angola became increasingly coordinated despite Soviet reluctance to become deeply involved in an area it regarded as being of little geopolitical significance.

Table 3

CUBAN TROOPS AND MILITARY ADVISORS IN AFRICA AND THE MIDDLE EAST, 1966-1980

Country	1966[a]	1974	1976	1977	1978	1980
Algeria	—	—	—	—	—	10-20
Angola	—	—	13,000	19,000	19,000	19,000
Benin	—	—	1000[b]	10-20	20	10-20
Congo-Brazzaville	700-1000	50-100	200-500[b]	300	500-600	300
Equatorial Guinea	—	80	—	150-200[d]	100[d]	10-20
Ethiopia	—	—	25-300[b]	60-120	16,000-17,000	13,000-15,000
Guinea-Bissau	—	—	150	300-500	100-150	50
Guinea-Conakry	50-100	200	—	150	400-500	10-20
Iraq	—	—	—	100-125	20	10-20
Libya	—	—	1200	30	200	—
Madagascar	—	—	20-25	650-750	—	200-300
Mozambique	—	—	50-1500[c]	120-125	1000	10-20
Sierra Leone	—	10-25	200	200	10-15	—
Somalia	—	—	500	—	—	—
South Yemen	—	600-700	—	—	300-400	300-400
Tanzania	—	150	—	25[d]	50	—
Uganda	—	—	—	—	60[d]	—
Zambia	—	—	—	—	15-60[e]	100

Table 3 (cont.)

Country	1966[a]	1974	1976	1977	1978	1980
TOTAL	750-1100	1090-1255	17,120-17,900	21,495-21,950	37,775-39,175	33,010-35,260
Average per Country	375-550	180-210	1555-1625	1535-1566	2518-2612	2539-2712
TOTAL excl. Angola and Ethiopia	750-1100	1090-1255	4120-4900	2095-2550	2775-3175	1010-1260
Average per Country	375-550	180-210	412-490	175-213	213-244	92-115

Sources: 1966, 1974: William J. Durch, *The Cuban Military in Africa and the Middle East* [Professional Paper No. 201] (Arlington, Va.: Center for Naval Analysis, 1977); *1976:* Western intelligence sources as cited in U.S. press; see esp. *Washington Star,* January 22, 1976, and *Christian Science Monitor,* February 23, 1977; *1977:* U.S. National Security Council estimates as reported in *Washington Post,* November 18, 1977; *1978:* Western intelligence sources as cited in *Newsweek,* March 13, 1978; *1980:* Western intelligence sources as compiled from press reports and government press releases.

[a]1966 marked the highpoint of the Cuban presence during the 1960s.

[b]Staging and trans-shipment points for Angola.

[c]Indicates expansion of Cuban presence in Somalia during 1976 rather than margin of error in estimation.

[d]In December 1977, Castro denied that Cuba had any military advisors in Uganda, and put the number in Equatorial Guinea at 8-10 rather than 150-200 estimated in the November 1977 NSC report (see *New York Times,* December 7, 1977).

[e]Covertly training guerrillas of the Zimbabwe Patriotic Front and/or SWAPO.

In Ethiopia, Cuban-Soviet cooperation developed sooner and was far more extensive than in Angola. Both nations sought to achieve a negotiated settlement to create an anti-imperialist federation in the Horn, and from at least March 1977 onward, this aim was pursued jointly. When their diplomatic efforts collapsed, Cuba and the USSR cooperated in providing extensive military aid to Ethiopia.

The evolution of Cuba's African policy demonstrates quite clearly that its interventions in Angola and Ethiopia were logical extensions of Cuba's historic policy of providing international assistance to progressive forces abroad. Cuban policies have evolved independently, and despite their compatibility and increasing coordination with Soviet policies, they are different both in concept and application. Cuba is not the Soviet Union's proxy in Africa; the two are partners, and though the partnership is asymmetrical, it is reciprocal nonetheless. Through cooperation, each partner is able to attain policy objectives which neither could attain if acting alone.

The internal dynamics of such a partnership tend to impel it toward ever closer cooperation. So long as joint ventures are successful, each partner has an incentive to perpetuate and extend the partnership by reducing areas of policy conflict, which enables each partner to exercise some influence over the policies of the other. Such reciprocal leverage can be seen at several points in the Cuban-Soviet relationship. Cuban militance in Angola drew the USSR more deeply into the Angolan civil war than Soviet policymakers probably would have preferred, whereas in Ethiopia the intense Soviet interest in the Horn's geopolitics probably helped to deepen the Cuban involvement.

However, the prospects for joint ventures are limited by the degree of congruence between the policies of the two partners. Thus far the partnership has also been limited in scope by the reactive character of the two major interventions. While coordination has been high in response to crisis, it has not yet extended to the partners' long-term civilian or military assistance programs. Despite their cooperation in Angola and Ethiopia, there is little evidence that Cuba and the USSR are pursuing a jointly formulated "grand design" of continental scope in Africa. Though Cuban involvement in Africa expanded--both in terms of military and civilian economic assistance missions--in the wake of Angola, it has been relatively constant since 1976 (see Tables 3 and 4). Excluding Angola and Ethiopia, the total number of Cuban military advisors in Africa, the number of major military missions, and the average mission size have actually decreased.

Table 4

CUBAN CIVILIAN ADVISORS IN AFRICA AND THE MIDDLE EAST,
1977-1980

Country	1977	1980
Algeria	35	—
Angola	4000	6000-9000
Cape Verde Island	10-15	10-15
Congo-Brazzaville	15-25	200-275
Equatorial Guinea	150-200	50-100
Ethiopia	150	500-600
Guinea-Bissau	30-60	40-50
Iraq	350-400	1000
Mali	—	6
Mozambique	150	400-500
São Tomé & Principe	—	100-500
South Yemen	100	100-200
Tanzania	350-500	80
TOTAL	5340-5635	8486-12226

Source: Western intelligence sources as compiled from press reports.

Furthermore, a comparison of Cuban and Soviet aid missions (both civilian and military) in Africa shows no significant relationship (either positive or negative) in how they are distributed. That is to say, a nation with a Soviet aid mission is no more likely (or *less* likely) to have a Cuban mission than any other nation.[9] If Cuban and Soviet cooperation were premised on a "grand design" rather than being merely an ad hoc response to crises, one would expect to find some evidence of coordination in their military and/or civilian aid programs outside Angola and Ethiopia. The lack of such evidence, combined with the reactive nature of both the Angolan and Ethiopian interventions, suggests that Cuba and the USSR have not developed a joint overall strategy of military activism in Africa.[10] Their intervention and the extent of their cooperation depends upon the development of opportune situations; thus the prospect of future Cuban interventions depends primarily upon the course of events in Africa itself.

C. THE U.S. POLICY RESPONSE

U.S. policy toward Cuba's involvement in Africa has been worse than ineffectual. In both Angola and Ethiopia, U.S. policy positively contributed to the escalation of conflict, helping to create the necessary conditions for close Cuban-Soviet collaboration and successful Cuban intervention. U.S. covert aid to the FNLA subverted the Alvor Agreements in Angola, thereby initiating the internationalization of the civil war. Once Cuban troops began arriving in Angola, the United States could have prevented an MPLA victory only by joining openly with South Africa. In the Horn, U.S. attempts to wean Somalia from the Soviet camp with an offer of "defensive arms" were interpreted by the Somalis, however inaccurately, as U.S. acquiescence to a full-scale invasion of the Ogaden. Once Cuban troops began arriving in Ethiopia, the United States could have prevented Somalia's defeat only by implicitly endorsing Somali aggression with U.S. military aid. In both cases, the ineptitude of U.S. policy provided Cuba and the USSR with opportunities to intervene on the "right" side (i.e., with substantial regional support), while leaving U.S. policymakers with the Hobson's choice of openly backing the "wrong" side or disengaging. Ironically, the policies which created these predicaments were both premised on reducing Soviet influence in the region.

Making no distinction between Cuban and Soviet policies, U.S. policy has centered on preventing future interventions by threatening the global interests of the USSR, and by basing U.S. regional policies upon the imperative of containing Cuban and Soviet influence. The global dimension of this response initially had both diplomatic and military aspects: the United States threatened to dismantle detente and/or react militarily to any future Soviet-Cuban activism in Africa. Neither of these policy approaches was particularly satisfactory. To the extent that detente was mutually beneficial to the superpowers, many U.S. officials argued against linkage between local tensions and global rivalries on the grounds that the stakes in U.S.-Soviet bilateral relations were too high to allow regional issues to be controlling factors. With respect to Cuba, the absence of diplomatic and economic relations between the United States and Cuba severely limited U.S. leverage. The United States could attempt to use the prospect of normalizing relations as an incentive for Cuban restraint, but Cuba was unlikely to abandon its highly successful African policy in exchange for a few hundred million dollars worth of trade with the United States.

The prospects for a U.S. military response to Cuban and Soviet involvement were equally dim. Regional support for Cuba and the Soviet Union, combined with domestic resistance in the United States to involvement in "another Vietnam," made a major U.S.

military response unfeasible. In short, efforts to deter Cuban and Soviet involvement in Africa failed because the United States did not have sufficient leverage with either country to make the strategy effective.

With the deterioration of detente and the coming of the new cold war, the prospects for inducing Soviet restraint by diplomatic means have greatly diminished. If the Soviet Union's reticence to become deeply involved in the Angolan civil war was due to fears that detente might be damaged, that potential cost no longer has to be weighed. Should war erupt in Namibia, for example, it is difficult to imagine what diplomatic incentive the Soviet Union would have for restraint.

The regional dimension of the U.S. response was typified by Henry Kissinger's attempt to promote a "moderate solution" in Rhodesia by freezing the supposedly pro-Soviet Patriotic Front out of the new majority government. This was not a regional policy which neatly integrated global and regional interests: it was a policy with a globalist pivot behind a regionalist facade. U.S. interests in Rhodesia were still being viewed through the prism of East-West antagonisms. In fact this was essentially the same policy pursued in Angola, where the United States tried to deprive the MPLA of any role in the post-independence government. The only difference lay in method: in Angola it was covert action; in Rhodesia it was diplomacy. After initial proclamations that it would no longer subordinate regional policy to globalism, the Carter administration drifted back into more traditional patterns, as its responses in Ethiopia, Zaire, Yemen, and the Western Sahara bear witness.

British policy toward Zimbabwe offers a stark contrast. When the United States was on the verge of lifting sanctions against the Muzorewa government (thus threatening to prolong the guerrilla war and thoroughly discredit U.S. policy in the region), even the conservative Thatcher government had the sense to recognize that Muzorewa could only survive through a negotiated settlement that included the Patriotic Front. The Lancaster House agreements improved the prospects for a peaceful settlement while enhancing British prestige in the area. The United States can point to no comparable policy success in Africa.

On the contrary, the United States has paid a heavy political price for its African policy. Its singular concern with Cuban and Soviet influence reinforces African suspicions that the United States is only superficially concerned with African realities. Given Africa's colonial history, it is not surprising that Africans resent being treated like pawns on the chessboard of Great Power rivalries. Both Cuba and the Soviet Union are extremely sensitive to these feelings, being careful to intervene only when the overwhelming consensus of regional opinion is in their favor. The United States, meanwhile, is busy propping up such paragons as Mobutu, and posturing against external intervention while maintaining a deafening silence on French military presence in Africa. Is it any wonder that even Nigeria has begun to regard U.S. policy as hypocritical?

Though it has become fashionable to remonstrate about the sterility of the globalist/regionalist debate and the need to transcend it, the differences between these two perspectives are real ones. Even in their most sophisticated, least doctrinaire variants, they involve different estimations of the importance of regional forces in the development of conflicts, the ability of external actors to manipulate those forces with any prospect of securing long-term advantage, and the global impact of regional events. Such differences lead inexorably to different policy prescriptions.

Paradoxically, the most effective response to Cuban and Soviet intervention in Africa would be to stop allowing the prospect of interventions to distort U.S. policy. Nothing has been more responsible for the lack of a coherent U.S. policy toward Africa than the obsession with Cuban and Soviet involvement. The preoccupation with the Cuban-Soviet role provides the comforting illusion of coherent policy where there is none, leaving the United States with a conglomeration of ineffective and unrealistic initiatives which do more damage to U.S. interests than any Soviet or Cuban successes. The United States must begin to address the complexities of regional issues with carefully crafted policies based upon a clearly defined set of U.S. interests, of which the containment of Soviet influence is only one.

U.S. attempts to avert further Cuban interventions in Africa will be futile unless they are integrated into such a comprehensive policy. Within that context, however, it is possible to outline a general strategy to minimize the prospect of new Cuban military interventions on the scale of Angola or Ethiopia. When regional conflicts are resolved peacefully, as in Zimbabwe, there is no opportunity for Cuba or the Soviet Union to intervene. If the United States had followed a policy of facilitating a peaceful solution in Angola, it would have pressured the FNLA to abide by the Alvor Agreements instead of providing Roberto with the arms to overturn them.

When regional conflicts erupt in violence, U.S. policy should be aimed at minimizing *all* external intervention, and especially its escalation. Angola and Ethiopia demonstrated that Cuban and Soviet policies are essentially reactive; while they did not initiate the internationalization of those conflicts, Cuba and the Soviets were prepared to match escalation for escalation. By limiting the internationalization of regional conflicts, the United States can probably preclude major Cuban or Soviet interventions by depriving them of their legitimacy. In southern Africa, the United States should exert pressure to deter Pretoria from a major military intervention in Zimbabwe even if the new regime gives sanctuary to guerrillas operating in South Africa.

These basic policies can be supplemented with measures designed to directly discourage major Cuban and Soviet interventions. Such bilateral measures, however, must take cognizance of the differences between Cuban and Soviet policies, and should include incentives as well as sanctions. It must be understood that these will be effective only in marginal cases and only over a narrow range of Cuban or Soviet behavior; they will not prevent either country from coming to the aid of an ally under attack. Bilateral measures are likely to be more effective in inducing Cuban and Soviet cooperation in resolving regional conflicts short of violence than in deterring Cuban-Soviet intervention.

This sort of cooperation would be greatly facilitated if the United States had normal diplomatic relations with Cuba. The existence of regular diplomatic channels might also prevent such misunderstandings (if they can charitably be called that) as the U.S. confusion over Cuba's role in the 1978 Shaba invasion and the 1979 Soviet brigade crisis. Normalizing relations would also provide the United States with at least *some* leverage over Cuban behavior, where it now has none.

Finally, in those cases where Cuban and Soviet interventions have already occurred, U.S. policy should be aimed at building normal, constructive relations with the regimes in power as rapidly as possible. While this would mean contributing to the stabilization of the socialist regimes in Angola and Ethiopia, it would also mean a speedier withdrawal of Cuban troops, thereby lessening the dependence of those governments on Cuban and Soviet military aid. Given the clear Soviet and Cuban commitments to the security of Angola and Ethiopia, it is unrealistic to hope for a change in the status quo. Certain U.S. policies could undoubtedly "raise the cost" of the Cuban-Soviet commitments and delay the stabilization of the Angolan and Ethiopian regimes, but this would only serve to increase their dependence and intensify their anti-Americanism; it would not cause their downfall. Such policies may be viscerally gratifying, but as the history of U.S.-Cuban relations demonstrates, they are not very effective. As various "roads to socialism" proliferate, the United States must learn to make finer distinctions between national communisms. There is no reason why a nation which abolishes private enterprise must necessarily become an implacable foe of the United States or an unshakable ally of the Soviet Union. But if U.S. policy treats nations in that way, they will certainly become so.

Cuba's recent policy in Africa has been consistent with the policies of the 1960s, independent of Soviet control, and reactive to the threats faced by Cuba's friends abroad. Since Cuba's new activism is a logical application of well-established policies, it is unlikely to change radically in the foreseeable future, nor is it apt to be responsive to U.S. pressure. The consistency of Cuban policy, however, makes it possible to project potential applications in a variety of future circumstances. Cuba will continue to supply arms and advisors to national liberation movements, but it is unlikely to deploy regular combat troops except in defense of existing progressive governments under foreign attack. The role Cuba ultimately plays in southern Africa will depend partly upon the limits of Cuba's partnership with the Soviet Union and partly upon what role Africans themselves want Cuba to play. More fundamentally, though, it will depend upon the intransigence of South Africa. Unless the Zimbabwe solution can be replicated, the guerrilla wars in southern Africa will intensify, and in turn will increase the guerrillas' dependency upon a growing Cuban and Soviet presence.

The greatest danger for the United States is that its preoccupation with Cuba will lead it to enlist on the side of regimes which are neither stable nor popular (as in Zaire and Yemen), or on the side of international causes which are widely regarded as illegitimate (as in the Ogaden and the Western Sahara). The renewal of the cold war will undoubtedly intensify this tendency around the globe, as it has already in southwest Asia (the new U.S. relationship with Zia's Pakistan being the principal example). Even if such policies are successful in the short run, their long-term consequences for U.S. interests will be dire. Military assistance creates only the facade of stability where there is none; it does not make an illegitimate government legitimate. On the contrary, it provides unsound regimes with the wherewithal to resist the domestic changes that are requisite to real stability. To pursue a policy of propping up governments indiscriminately whenever and wherever the precepts of cold war geopolitics appear to dictate is to build castles in the sand. Eventually the tide will come in.

NOTES

Chapter I

1. For more detailed discussion of Cuban-Soviet relations, see Edward Gonzalez: "Castro's Revolution, Cuban Communist Appeals, and the Soviet Response," *World Politics* 21, 1 (October 1968): 39-68, and "Relationship with the Soviet Union," in *Revolutionary Change in Cuba,* ed. Carmelo Mesa-Lago (Pittsburgh: University of Pittsburgh Press, 1971), pp. 81-105; Leon Goure and Julian Weinkle, "Soviet-Cuban Relations: The Growing Integration," in *Cuba, Castro, and Revolution,* ed. Jaime Suchlicki (Coral Gables: University of Miami Press, 1972), pp. 144-89; D. Bruce Jackson, *Castro, the Kremlin, and Communism in Latin America* (Baltimore: Johns Hopkins Press, 1969); Lynn D. Bender, *The Politics of Hostility* (Hato Rey, Puerto Rico: Inter-American University Press, 1975). The thesis that Cuba is acting as a proxy for the Soviet Union in Africa is developed in Brian Crozier, "The Surrogate Forces of the Soviet Union," *Conflict Studies* 92 (February 1978): 1-20.

2. For details on this period, see Carmelo Mesa-Lago: "Economic Policies and Growth," in Mesa-Lago, ed., pp. 277-340, and "Ideological, Political, and Economic Factors in the Cuban Controversy on Material vs. Moral Incentives," *Journal of Latin American Studies and World Affairs* 14 (February 1972): 49-111; Archibald R. M. Ritter, *The Economic Development of Revolutionary Cuba* (New York: Praeger, 1974).

3. Jackson, pp. 90-91.

4. David E. Albright, "The USSR and Africa: Soviet Policy," *Problems of Communism* 27, 1 (January-February 1978): 20-39.

5. See, for example, Jorge I. Dominguez, *Cuba: Order and Revolution* (Cambridge: Harvard University Press, 1978), pp. 162-65.

6. Castro's speech is reprinted in *Granma Weekly Review,* August 25, 1968, pp. 1-4.

7. Carmelo Mesa-Lago, *Cuba in the 1970s* (Albuquerque: University of New Mexico Press, 1978), pp. 30-61.

8. *Ibid.,* pp. 116-45; Jorge I. Dominguez, "Taming the Cuban Shrew," *Foreign Policy* 10 (Spring 1973): 94-116. For an excellent chronology of these events, see Barry A. Sklar, *Cuba: Normalization of Relations* (Congressional Research Service Issue Brief Number IB75030; Washington, D.C.: Library of Congress, 1977).

9. *Ibid.*

Chapter II

1. William J. Durch has prepared an excellent summary of Cuban military assistance programs in Africa prior to Angola: *The Cuban Military in Africa and*

the *Middle East* (Professional Paper No. 201; Arlington, Va.: Center for Naval Analysis, 1977). See also Nelson Valdes, "Revolutionary Solidarity in Angola," in *Cuba in the World*, eds. Cole Blaiser and Carmelo Mesa-Lago (Pittsburgh: University of Pittsburgh Press, 1979), pp. 87-118.

2. Ernesto Guevara, *Che: Selected Works of Ernesto Guevara*, edited by Rolando E. Bonachea and Nelson P. Valdes (Cambridge: MIT Press, 1969), pp. 350-62.

3. *Ibid.*, "Introduction," pp. 25-27.

4. Gabriel García-Marquez, "Operation Carlota," *New Left Review* 101-102 (February-April 1977): 123-37; Valdes, p. 92.

5. Durch also makes this point (Durch, p. 20).

6. *Ibid.*, pp. 20-24; Valdes, pp. 92-93; *Africa Report*, October 1966, p. 32.

7. Valdes, p. 95.

8. On the changes in Soviet policy, see Albright, pp. 25f; Iri Valenta, "The Soviet-Cuban Intervention in Angola, 1975," *Studies in Comparative Communism* 11, 1-2 (Spring-Summer 1978): 6-7; Jacques Levesque, *The USSR and the Cuban Revolution* (New York: Praeger, 1978). For Guevara's complaint, see Guevara, pp. 350-62.

9. George T. Yu, "The USSR and Africa: China's Impact," *Problems of Communism* 27, 1 (January-February 1978): 40-50.

10. Durch, pp. 25-26.

11. *Ibid.*, pp. 27-31.

Chapter III

1. *Ibid.*

2. García-Marquez, pp. 126-27; Danny Schecter, "The Havana-Luanda Connection," *Cuba Review* 6, 1 (March 1976): 5-13; John A. Marcum, *The Angolan Revolution: Exile Politics and Guerrilla Warfare, 1962-1976* (Cambridge: MIT Press, 1978), pp. 224-25.

3. Richard Gibson, *African Liberation Movements* (New York: Oxford University Press, 1972), pp. 208-17; Marcum, *passim*.

4. *Ibid.*, pp. 276-77.

5. Marcum, pp. 185-240; Gibson, pp. 222-23.

6. Immanuel Wallerstein, "Luanda is Madrid," *The Nation*, January 3-10, 1976.

7. Marcum, pp. 162-67, 193-95, 276-77.

8. *Ibid.*, pp. 10, 22f.

9. *New York Times*, September 25, 1975.

10. Durch, pp. 63n, 105.

11. Marcum, p. 240.

12. *Ibid.*, pp. 171-72. For a history of Soviet-MPLA relations, see Christopher Stevens, "The Soviet Union and Angola," *African Affairs* 75, 229 (April 1976): 137-51.

13. Basil Davidson et al., *Southern Africa: The New Politics of Revolution* (New York: Penguin, 1976), pp. 83-84.

14. Colin Legum, "A Study of Foreign Intervention," in *After Angola: The War Over Southern Africa*, eds. C. Legum and Tony Hodges (London: Rex Collings, 1976), p. 11.

15. Davidson, pp. 85-86; John Stockwell, *In Search of Enemies: A CIA Story* (New York: Norton, 1978).

16. Valenta, pp. 14-16; Colin Legum, "The Soviet Union, China, and the West in Southern Africa," *Foreign Affairs* 54, 4 (July 1976): 746-62.

17. Valenta.

18. The Soviets supported the agreements reached at Alvor; see Valenta, p. 10.

19. Seymour Hersh in *New York Times*, December 19, 1975; Marcum, pp. 257-59; Valdes, p. 9.

20. See, for example, Marcum, p. 273, and Durch, pp. 41-42. But García-Marquez, in his authorized account, reports that the first delegation of instructors arrived in early October (p. 124).

21. Marcum, pp. 262, 271.

22. *Ibid.*; Stockwell.

23. Marcum, pp. 266-69.

24. *Ibid.*, p. 443n257.

25. *Ibid.*; García-Marquez, p. 124.

26. Marcum, p. 273.

27. García-Marquez, pp. 127-28, 136. Marcum, however, estimates that as many as 1,500 Cubans were in Angola in October *(personal correspondence)*.

28. Fidel Castro, "Angola: African Giron," *Granma Weekly Review*, April 18, 1976.

29. García-Marquez, p. 128. *New York Times*, February 5, 1976, reported the following comment from a Soviet official: "We did not twist their arms. The Cubans wanted to go in . . . . They are more radical than we are." Kissinger's views are reported in the same article.

30. Stevens, pp. 143-45. On the factors involved in the Soviet decision to intervene, see Valenta, pp. 19ff.

31. *Ibid.*; Durch, pp. 48-49.

32. *Washington Post*, April 10, 1977.

33. Dominguez, p. 354; *Granma Weekly Review*, August 8, 1976, p. 3.

34. Gerald J. Bender, "Angola, the Cubans, and American Anxieties," *Foreign Policy* 31 (Summer 1978): 3-33; *New York Times*, November 13, 1977.

35. See the accounts of the invasion in *Washington Post*, March 17 and 22, 1977.

36. Fidel Castro as quoted in *Washington Post*, March 22, 1977.

37. Sklar, pp. 18-19.

38. Bender, pp. 14-15; *International Bulletin*, March 28, 1977.

39. See Bender's account of the coup attempt (Bender, pp. 23-26) and Basil David- son, "Angola Since Independence," *Race and Class* 19, 2 (1977): 133-48.

40. *Ibid.*, p. 26; *New York Times*, December 14, 1978.

41. *Ibid.; Washington Post*, December 15, 1978.

42. Barbara Walters, "An Interview with Fidel Castro," *Foreign Policy* 28 (Fall 1977), and Castro's conversation with U.S. press, *New York Times*, December 7, 1977.

43. For an exceptional report of UNITA activity by a reporter who accompa- nied the guerrillas inside Angola for several months, see Leon Dash, " A Long March in Angola," *Washington Post*, August 7-13, 1977.

44. "1978 Chronology," *Southern Africa* 11, 9 (December 1978): 21-23.

45. *International Bulletin*, July 31, 1978; *Washington Post*, May 15, 1978; *New York Times*, May 22, 1978.

46. *New York Times*, May 19, 1978; June 11, 1978; June 14, 1978.

47. *New York Times*, May 26, 1978; *Washington Post*, June 14, 1978.

48. On the Senate committee's doubts, see *New York Times*, May 27, 1978; *Washington Post*, May 27, 1978; *Washington Star*, June 10, 1978. On doubts in the House committee, see *Washington Post*, June 9, 1978. On doubts within the Administration, see *Washington Post*, June 5, 1978; *Christian Science Monitor*, June 8, 1978.

49. For the course of this debate, see *Washington Star*, May 30, 1978; *Washing- ton Post*, June 1, 1978; *New York Times* and *Washington Post*, June 5 and June 14, 1978.

50. "1978 Chronology," pp. 21-23.

51. For a review of Zaire's current predicaments, see Leon Dash's three-part series in *Washington Post*, December 30 and 31, 1979, and January 1, 1980.

52. *International Bulletin*, August 28, 1978.

53. On the South African border raids, see *Washington Post*, November 1, 1979. On the implications of Neto's death, see *Washington Post*, September 12, 1979.

54. García-Marquez, pp. 127-28.

55. Sklar, p. 31.

56. U.S. Congress, House, Committee on International Relations, Subcommittee on Inter-American Affairs, *Impact of Cuban-Soviet Ties in the Western Hemisphere*, Testimony from the Defense Intelligence Agency, Hearings, 95th Cong., 2nd Sess., March 14, 15, April 5, 12, 1978 (Washington D.C.: U.S. GPO, 1978), pp. 2-3. See also *New York Times*, November 17, 1978; *Washington Post*, November 18, 1978.

57. See especially Fidel Castro's speech to the 1973 Nonaligned Conference in Algiers, *Granma Weekly Review*, September 16, 1973, p. 12. For a discus- sion of Cuba's role in the nonaligned movement, see William M. LeoGrande,

"The Evolution of the Nonaligned Movement," *Problems of Communism*, January-February 1980.

58. Abraham F. Lowenthal, "Cuba's African Adventure," *International Security* 2, 1 (Summer 1977): 3-10.

59. On Cuba's debt, see William M. LeoGrande, "Cuban Dependency," *Cuban Studies/Estudios Cubanos* 9, 2 (July 1979).

60. Sklar, p. 33; *International Bulletin*, March 26, 1976.

61. Jorge I. Dominguez, "The Cuban Operation in Angola: Costs and Benefits for the Armed Forces," *Cuban Studies/Estudios Cubanos* 8, 1 (January 1978): 10-21; Edward Gonzalez, "Complexities of Cuban Foreign Policy," *Problems of Communism* 26, 6 (November-December 1977): 1-15.

62. *Ibid.*

Chapter IV

1. Raúl Valdes Vivo, *Ethiopia's Revolution* (New York: International Publishers, 1978).

2. *Ibid.*

3. *New York Times*, November 14, 1977.

4. *Ibid.; Washington Post*, May 26, 1977.

5. *New York Times*, March 13, 1977.

6. *Ibid.*, November 14, 1977.

7. *Ibid.*, April 5, 1976.

8. See, for example, Valdes Vivo; Fidel Castro's interview in *Afrique-Asie*, March 29, 1967; Miguel F. Roa, "Para Defender la Revolución Etiope," *Verde Olivo* 13 (1977): 18-21.

9. Fidel Castro, speech of March 18, 1978; cited in *Granma Weekly Review*, March 19, 1978.

10. *New York Times*, March 13, 1977; *Washington Post*, March 18, 1977.

11. *International Bulletin*, March 28, 1977.

12. *Washington Post*, May 26, 1977; *New York Times*, June 21, 1977.

13. *Washington Post*, January 13 and February 2, 1978.

14. *Newsweek*, March 13, 1978; *New York Times*, February 8, 1978.

15. *New York Times*, February 14, 1978.

16. *Washington Post*, April 1, 1978.

17. *New York Times*, February 11 and 14, 1978; *Washington Post*, November 18, 1977; *International Bulletin*, January 30, 1978.

18. *Pravda* (Moscow), March 15, 1978.

19. *The Observer* (London), February 27, 1978.

20. *Granma Weekly Review*, August 13, 1978.

21. *The Guardian* (New York), July 12, 1978.

22. See the speeches by Castro and Mengistu reported in *Granma Weekly Review*, May 7, 1978.

23. *New York Times*, November 12, 1978; *Washington Post*, May 30, 1978.

24. *New York Times*, December 1, 1978.

25. *Ibid.*, November 12 and December 1, 1978.

26. *Los Angeles Times*, March 7, 1979; *Washington Post*, February 13, 1980.

27. *Ibid.*, February 5, 1980; *New York Times*, February 25, 1980.

28. *Ibid.*, July 20, 1978.

29. *Ibid.*, June 11 and July 26, 1978.

30. *Washington Post*, January 27, 1979.

31. *Miami Herald*, May 27 and June 2, 1978.

32. Carmelo Mesa-Lago and Sandra Miller, "Chronology of U.S.-Cuban Rapprochement: 1977," *Cuban Studies/Estudios Cubanos* 8, 1 (January 1978): 36-43.

33. Sklar, pp. 23-24; *New York Times*, January 2, 1979.

34. Donald S. Zagoria, "Into the Breach: New Soviet Alliances in the Third World," *Foreign Affairs* 57, 4 (Spring 1979): 733-54; Robert Legvold, "The Super Rivals: Conflict in The Third World," *Foreign Affairs* 57, 4 (Spring 1979): 755-78.

35. *New York Times*, November 17, 1978; *Washington Post*, November 18, 1978.

36. *New York Times*, January 16, 1978.

37. *Washington Post*, August 31 and September 1, 1979.

38. *Ibid.*

39. Vance declared the status quo "unacceptable" on September 5 (*New York Times*, September 6, 1979), and Carter repeated the phrase two days later (*Washington Post*, September 8, 1979).

40. See, for example, *Washington Post*, September 6 and October 16, 1979; *New York Times*, September 13, 1979.

41. For the Soviet position, see the editorial in *Pravda*, September 10, 1979, and Gromyko's speech to the United Nations reported in *New York Times*, September 26, 1979. For the Cuban view, see Fidel Castro's interview with U.S. journalists reported in *Granma Weekly Review*, October 7, 1979.

42. *New York Times*. September 13, 1979.

43. The text of Carter's speech is in *New York Times*, October 2, 1979. On the Guantanamo landing, see *New York Times*, October 18, 1979; *Washington Post*, October 6, 1979.

Chapter V

1. *Impact of Cuban Soviet Ties in the Western Hemisphere,* pp. 2ff.

2. Durch, pp. 31-33.

3. Sklar, pp. 23, 31.

4. *Ibid.,* p. 18.

5. *Washington Post,* March 22, 1977.

6. *New York Times,* December 17, 1978.

7. *International Bulletin,* May 21, 1976.

8. *Washington Post,* February 1, 1980.

9. The twists and turns of U.S. policy on the UN sanctions are reported in *New York Times,* May 14 and May 17, 1979; *Washington Post,* August 10 and November 15, 1979. The best account of U.S. policy toward Rhodesia in the late 1960s and early 1970s is Anthony Lake, *The "Tar Baby" Option: American Policy Towards Southern Rhodesia* (New York: Columbia University Press, 1976).

10. *New York Times,* December 22, 1979.

11. *Washington Post,* December 22, 1979.

12. Gibson, pp. 181f.

13. See Castro's speech to the UN, *Granma Weekly Review,* October 21, 1979.

14. Durch, pp. 25-26.

15. Fred Halliday, "Yemen's Unfinished Revolution: Socialism in the South," *MERIP Reports* 81 (October 1979): 3-20.

16. *Ibid.,* pp. 16-19.

17. *New York Times,* May 25, 1979.

18. *New York Times,* February 26, 1979.

19. *Washington Post,* February 27, 1979.

20. *Ibid.,* March 7, 1979.

21. *Ibid.,* March 7 and 10, 1979; *New York Times,* March 8, 1979.

22. *Ibid.,* March 6, 1979.

23. *New York Times,* March 8, 1979.

24. *Washington Post,* March 10, 1979.

25. President Ali Abdullah Saleh accused both the United States and USSR of playing a "superpower game" in the region (*Washington Post,* March 10, 1979).

26. *New York Times,* March 20 and 28, 1979.

27. *Washington Post,* April 11, 1979.

28. *Ibid.,* January 31 and February 20, 1980.

29. Halliday; *New York Times,* March 29, 1979.

30. *Washington Post,* October 29, 1979.
31. *Ibid.,* October 18, 1979.
32. *New York Times,* February 18, 1980.
33. *Ibid.*

Chapter VI

1. For a fuller discussion of Cuba's role in the Nonaligned Movement, see Leo-Grande, "Evolution of the Nonaligned Movement."

2. "Declaration of the 5th Summit of Nonaligned Nations," *Foreign Broadcast Information Service Daily Report, Middle East and North Africa,* August 23-24, 1976.

3. LeoGrande, "Evolution of the Nonaligned Movement."

4. *Washington Post,* September 22, 1979.

5. *Ibid.,* January 11, 1980.

6. *Ibid.*

7. *Newsweek,* February 4, 1980.

8. For the text of the speech, see *Granma Weekly Review,* January 27, 1980.

9. Using data from *Communist Aid to Less Developed Countries of the Free World* (Washington, D.C.: CIA, 1978), tables 2 and 6. The Pearson correlation between Cuban and Soviet military missions (excluding Angola and Ethiopia) is r = -.19 (n = 11); between civilian aid missions, r = -.06 (n = 11). Neither is statistically significant.

10. Albright argues persuasively that the Soviet Union itself does not have a continental strategy in Africa. See also Legvold.

WILLIAM M. LEOGRANDE is Assistant Professor of Political Science, School of Government and Public Administration, The American University, Washington D.C. He received his Ph.D. from The Maxwell School, Syracuse University in 1976. He has contributed articles on Cuban politics and foreign policy, and on U.S. policy toward Latin America, to such journals as *Foreign Affairs, Journal of Inter-American Studies, Problems of Communism,* and *Latin American Research Review.*

INSTITUTE OF INTERNATIONAL STUDIES
UNIVERSITY OF CALIFORNIA, BERKELEY

215 Moses Hall   Berkeley, California 94720

CARL G. ROSBERG, *Director*

Monographs published by the Institute include:

RESEARCH SERIES

1. *The Chinese Anarchist Movement.* R.A. Scalapino and G.T. Yu. ($1.00)
7. *Birth Rates in Latin America.* O. Andrew Collver. ($2.50)
16. *The International Imperatives of Technology.* Eugene B. Skolnikoff. ($2.95)
19. *Entry of New Competitors in Yugoslav Market Socialism.* S.R. Sacks. ($2.50)
20. *Political Integration in French-Speaking Africa.* Abdul A. Jalloh. ($3.50)
21. *The Desert & the Sown: Nomads in Wider Society.* Ed. C. Nelson. ($5.50)
22. *U.S.-Japanese Competition in International Markets.* J.E. Roemer. ($3.95)
23. *Political Disaffection Among British Students.* J. Citrin and D.J. Elkins ($2.00)
24. *Urban Inequality and Housing Policy in Tanzania.* Richard E. Stren. ($2.95)
25. *The Obsolescence of Regional Integration Theory.* Ernst B. Haas. ($6.95)
26. *The Voluntary Service Agency in Israel.* Ralph M. Kramer. ($2.00)
27. *The SOCSIM Microsimulation Program.* E. A. Hammel et al. ($4.50)
28. *Authoritarian Politics in Communist Europe.* Ed. Andrew C. Janos. ($8.95)
30. *Plural Societies and New States.* Robert Jackson. ($2.00)
31. *Politics of Oil Pricing in the Middle East, 1970-75.* R.C. Weisberg. ($4.95)
32. *Agricultural Policy and Performance in Zambia.* Doris J. Dodge. ($4.95)
34. *Housing the Urban Poor in Africa.* Richard E. Stren. ($5.95)
35. *The Russian New Right: Right-Wing Ideologies in USSR.* A. Yanov. ($5.95)
36. *Social Change in Romania, 1860-1940.* Ed. Kenneth Jowitt. ($4.50)
37. *The Leninist Response to National Dependency.* Kenneth Jowitt. ($4.95)
38. *Socialism in Sub-Saharan Africa.* Eds. C. Rosberg & T. Callaghy. ($12.95)
39. *Tanzania's Ujamaa Villages: Rural Development Strategy.* D. McHenry. ($5.95)
40. *Who Gains from Deep Ocean Mining?* I.G. Bulkley. ($3.50)
41. *Industrialization & the Nation-State in Peru.* Frits Wils. ($5.95)
42. *Ideology, Public Opinion, & Welfare Policy.* R.M. Coughlin. ($6.50)
43. *The Apartheid Regime: Political Power and Racial Domination.* Eds. R.M. Price and C. G. Rosberg. ($12.50)
44. *Yugoslav Economic System in the 1970s.* Laura D. Tyson. ($5.95)
45. *Conflict in Chad.* Virginia Thompson & Richard Adloff. ($7.50)
46. *Conflict and Coexistence in Belgium.* Ed. Arend Lijphart. ($8.95)
47. *Changing Realities in Southern Africa.* Ed. Michael Clough. ($12.50)
48. *Nigerian Women Mobilized, 1900-1965.* Nina E. Mba. ($12.95)
49. *Institutions of Rural Development.* Eds. D. Leonard & D. Marshall. ($11.50)
50. *Politics of Women & Work in USSR & U.S.* Joel C. Moses. ($9.50)
51. *Zionism and Territory.* Baruch Kimmerling. ($12.50)
52. *Soviet Subsidization of Trade with East Europe.* M. Marrese/J. Vanous. ($14.50)
53. *Voluntary Efforts in Decentralized Management.* L. Ralston et al. ($9.00)

LIST OF PUBLICATIONS (continued)

54. *Corporate State Ideologies.* Carl Landauer. ($5.95)
55. *Effects of Economic Reform in Yugoslavia.* John P. Burkett. ($9.50)
56. *The Drama of the Soviet 1960s.* Alexander Yanov. ($8.50)
57. *Revolutions and Rebellions in Afghanistan.* Eds. M. Nazif Shahrani & Robert L. Canfield. ($14.95)
58. *Women Farmers of Malawi.* D. Hirschmann & M. Vaughan. ($8.95)
59. *Chilean Agriculture under Military Rule.* Lovell S. Jarvis. ($11.50)
60. *Influencing Political Behavior in Netherlands and Austria.* J. Houska. ($11.50)
61. *Social Policies in Western Industrial Societies.* C.F. Andrain. ($12.95)
62. *Comparative Social Policy.* Harold Wilensky et al. ($7.50)
63. *State-Building Failure in Ireland and Algeria.* I. Lustick. ($8.95)

POLICY PAPERS IN INTERNATIONAL AFFAIRS

1. *Images of Detente & the Soviet Political Order.* K. Jowitt. ($1.25)
2. *Detente After Brezhnev: Domestic Roots of Soviet Policy.* A. Yanov. ($4.50)
3. *Mature Neighbor Policy: A New Policy for Latin America.* A. Fishlow. ($3.95)
4. *Five Images of Soviet Future: Review & Synthesis.* G.W. Breslauer. ($4.50)
5. *Global Evangelism: How to Protect Human Rights.* E.B. Haas. ($2.95)
6. *Israel & Jordan: An Adversarial Partnership.* Ian Lustick. ($2.00)
7. *Political Syncretism in Italy.* Giuseppe Di Palma. ($3.95)
8. *U.S. Foreign Policy in Sub-Saharan Africa.* Robert M. Price. ($4.50)
9. *East-West Technology Transfer in Perspective.* R.J. Carrick. ($5.50)
11. *Toward Africanized Policy for Southern Africa.* R. Libby. ($7.50)
12. *Taiwan Relations Act & Defense of ROC.* Edwin K. Snyder et al. ($7.50)
13. *Cuba's Policy in Africa, 1959-1980.* William M. LeoGrande. ($4.50)
14. *Norway, NATO, & Forgotten Soviet Challenge.* K. Amundsen. ($3.95)
15. *Japanese Industrial Policy.* Ira Magaziner and Thomas Hout. ($6.50)
16. *Containment, Soviet Behavior, & Grand Strategy.* Robert Osgood. ($5.50)
17. *U.S.-Japanese Competition-Semiconductor Industry.* M. Borrus et al. ($7.50)
18. *Contemporary Islamic Movements in Perspective.* Ira Lapidus. ($4.95)
19. *Atlantic Alliance, Nuclear Weapons, & European Attitudes.* W. Thies. ($4.50)
20. *War and Peace: Views from Moscow & Beijing.* B. Garrett & B. Glaser. ($7.95)
21. *Emerging Japanese Economic Influence in Africa.* J. Moss & J. Ravenhill. ($8.95)
22. *Nuclear Waste Disposal under the Seabed.* Edward Miles et al. ($7.50)
23. *NATO: The Tides of Discontent.* Earl Ravenal. ($7.50)
24. *Power-Sharing in South Africa.* Arend Lijphart. ($10.00)
25. *Reassessing the Soviet Challenge in Africa.* Ed. M. Clough. ($8.00)
26. *Why We Still Need the United Nations.* Ernst Haas. ($8.50)

POLITICS OF MODERNIZATION SERIES

1. *Spanish Bureaucratic-Patrimonialism in America.* M. Sarfatti. ($2.00)
2. *Civil-Military Relations in Argentina, Chile, & Peru.* L. North. ($2.00)
9. *Modernization & Bureaucratic-Authoritarianism: Studies in South American Politics.* Guillermo O'Donnell. ($8.95)